# TwinPack
## Mallorca

**TONY KELLY**

Tony Kelly first visited Mallorca on a walking holiday in 1995 and he has been returning to the island ever since. In 2000 he was awarded a diploma by the Mallorca Tourist Board for his writing 'reflecting the true spirit and diverse nature of Mallorca'. An expert on Spain, his other guidebooks include *AA Essential Menorca*, *Essential Costa Brava* and *Spiral Gran Canaria*. He lives near Cambridge with his wife and young son.

If you have any comments or suggestions for this guide you can contact the editor at *Twinpacks@theAA.com*

**AA Publishing**
Find out more about AA Publishing and the wide range of travel publications and services the AA provides by visiting our website at *www.theAA.com/travel*

# Contents

## life *5–12*

A Personal View *6–7*

A Chronology *10–11*

Mallorca in Figures *8*

Best of Mallorca *12*

People of Mallorca *9*

## how to organise your time *13–22*

Walks and Drives *14–19*

What's On *22*

Finding Peace & Quiet *20–21*

## top 25 sights *23–48*

**1** Alcúdia *24*

**17** Port de Pollença *40*

**2** Artà *25*

**18** Puig de Randa *41*

**3** Badia de Palma *26*

**19** S'Albufera *42*

**4** Cap de Formentor *27*

**20** Sa Calobra *43*

**5** Castell d'Alaró *28*

**21** Serra de Tramuntana *44*

**6** Coves d'Artà *29*

**22** Sineu *45*

**7** Deià *30*

**23** Sóller *46*

**8** Fundació Pilar i Joan Miró *31*

**24** Son Marroig *47*

**9** La Granja *32*

**25** Valldemossa *48*

**10** Lluc *33*

**11** Palma *34*

**12** Palma's Castell de Bellver *35*

**13** Palma's Fundació la Caixa *36*

**14** Palma's La Seu *37*

**15** Palma's Palau
de l'Almudaina *38*

**16** Pollença *39*

Index *92–93*

# About this book 4

## best 49–60

Small Towns and Villages 50–51
Hermitages and Sacred Sites 52
Historic Sites 53
Resorts 54–55
Children's Activities 56–57

Scenic Places 58
Free Attractions 59
Places to Have Lunch 60

## where to... 61–83

**EAT AND DRINK**
In Palma 62–63
Around the Island 64–69

**STAY**
In Palma 70
Around the Island 71–73

**SHOP**
Markets 74
Shopping in Palma 75

Arts and Crafts in Palma 76
Arts and Crafts Around the Island 77

**BE ENTERTAINED**
Theatres and Concerts 78
Bars 79
Discos and Dinner Shows 80
Golf Courses 81
Watersports 82
Spectator Sports 83

## practical matters 85–91

Before you go 86
When you are there 87–91
Public transport 89

Personal safety 90
Health 90
Language 91

Credits, Acknowledgements and Titles in this Series 94

# About this book

## KEY TO SYMBOLS

✚ Grid reference to the Top 25 locator map

✉ Address

☎ Telephone number

🕐 Opening times

🍴 Restaurant or café on premises or nearby

🚉 Nearest railway station

🚌 Nearest bus route

⛴ Nearest riverboat or ferry stop

♿ Facilities for visitors with disabilities

✋ Admission charge

↔ Other nearby places of interest

❓ Tours, lectures or special events

➤ Indicates the page where you will find a fuller description

ℹ Tourist information

**TwinPack Mallorca** is divided into six sections to cover the six most important aspects of your visit to Mallorca. It includes:

- The author's view of the island and its people
- Suggested walks and excursions
- The top 25 sights to visit
- Features about different aspects of the island that make it special
- Detailed listings of restaurants, hotels, shops and nightlife
- Practical information

In addition, easy-to-read side panels provide fascinating extra facts and snippets, highlights of places to visit and invaluable practical advice.

### CROSS-REFERENCES
To help you make the most of your visit, cross-references, indicated by ➤, show you where to find additional information about a place or subject.

### MAPS
**The fold-out map** in the wallet at the back of the book is a large-scale island map of Mallorca.
**The Top 25 locator maps** found on the inside front and back covers of the book itself are for quick reference. They show the Top 25 Sights, described on pages 24–48, which are clearly plotted by number (**1**–**25**, not page number) in alphabetical order.

### PRICES
Where appropriate, an indication of the cost of an establishment is given by € signs: €€€ denotes higher prices, €€ denotes average prices, while € denotes lower charges.

# MALLORCA
## life

A Personal View *6–7*

Mallorca in Figures *8*

People of Mallorca *9*

A Chronology *10–11*

Best of Mallorca *12*

# A Personal View

You probably think you know Mallorca already. It is, after all, Europe's favourite holiday island, visited by over 8 million tourists a year. Its popular image abroad is of high-rise concrete resorts overrun by British and German tourists, who spend all day on the beach and all evening in the bars, where the food and the beer taste exactly the same as at home.

Don't tell everybody, but Mallorca is just not like that. Yes, it has its ugly pockets, but these are easily avoided and most of the holiday resorts are a lot more restrained than you expect. The tourists are confined to a few crowded ghettoes on the coast while the rest of the island gets on with its life. Mallorca has mountains, pretty villages, monasteries, market towns, nature reserves, fishing ports and even one or two quiet beaches. And in its capital, Palma, it has one of the finest cities in Spain.

Of course, nowhere in Mallorca is untouched by tourism. Tourists have been visiting the island ever since Frédéric Chopin and George Sand spent the winter in Valldemossa in 1838. In an early sign of the tensions to come, Sand fell out with the locals over her foreign manners and morals. More than a century later, in the 1950s and 1960s, Mallorca was the birthplace of the Mediterranean package holiday and the islanders had to get used to everything from hippies to topless sunbathing. Fishing villages were destroyed to make way for soulless hotels, and unspoilt stretches of coastline were defaced by hastily built 'urbanisations'.

*Visitors to Cala Guya bask in the hot sun*

The island that led the way into mass tourism is now leading the way out. Mallorca has had enough of the so-called 'lager louts' who only want to get sunburnt and drunk as cheaply as possible. These days the island is developing a new image, as an upmarket destination for walking, golf and rural tourism. Cheap and cheerful is out, chic and cultured is in.

In truth, Mallorca has always appealed to a wide variety of visitors. The Spanish royal family spend their summer holidays here. Britain's Prince Charles is a frequent visitor, as was the late Princess Diana. Among the many foreign celebrities to have, or are acquiring homes on the island are actor Michael Douglas, singer Annie Lennox, model Claudia Schiffer and racing driver Michael Schumacher. At the same time, Mallorca remains the favourite destination of millions of ordinary families, who know it as the best place in the Mediterranean for an old-fashioned seaside holiday.

Summer or winter, there is always something new to discover. You can walk in the mountains of the Serra de Tramuntana, where the air is scented with wild rosemary and pine. You can seek out chocolate-box villages, climb to hilltop castles, or explore the network of Roman roads which criss-crosses the central plain. Best of all, you can go where no guidebook leads you, leaving the coast far behind and venturing off the beaten track to discover those hidden towns and villages which are the essence of the authentic, timeless Mallorca.

**JOGGING ROUND MAJORCA**

One of the earliest foreign visitors to Mallorca was the English writer Gordon West, whose book *Jogging Round Majorca*, published in 1929, captures the quaint charms of a largely rustic island. He wrote: 'Gazing down the steep, rock-strewn slopes…one dreads the inevitable day when the passing of some Lord Brougham will change the coast into a place of villas and casinos, of elaborate hotels and fashionable clothes.'

*The almond orchards of Andratx, with the Sierra de Tramuntana behind*

7

# Mallorca in Figures

**GEOGRAPHY**
- Mallorca is the largest of the Balearic Islands, a group that includes Menorca, Ibiza and Formentera.
- Mallorca measures 100km from east to west and 75km from north to south.
- Mallorca lies 200km south of Barcelona off the east coast of Spain.
- Mallorca has 555km of coastline and 80 beaches.
- Palma averages a daily maximum temperature of 21.4°C, and seven hours of sunshine per day throughout the year.

**PEOPLE**
- Of some 800,000 people in Mallorca, about half live in the capital Palma. The next biggest towns are Manacor (35,000) and Inca (25,000). The population has doubled since 1950 and includes a large number of expatriates – most of whom are German and British.

**TOURISM**
- Mallorca received 1 million tourists in 1966, 3 million in 1978 and 8.802 million in 2005, of whom 39.3% were from Germany, 25.9% from Britain and 16% from mainland Spain.
- On busy days in summer up to 700 flights land at Palma airport, carrying up to 100,000 passengers.
- Mallorca has 286.000 hotel beds and 60,000 in tourist apartments.
- Mallorca has enough restaurant tables for a quarter of the population to eat out every night.
- Mallorca's GDP (Gross Domestic Product) per capita is more than 50% above the Spanish average. Two-thirds of the population work in tourism, which represents about 60% of GDP.

**LANGUAGE**
- The official languages are Catalan and Castilian Spanish; Catalan is now the preferred language in education and local government.
- Most people speak Mallorquín, a dialect of Catalan.

# People of Mallorca

### Ramón Llull
Ramón Llull (1235–1316) was a wealthy courtier in Palma until a disastrous seduction attempt led him to retire to Puig de Randa in isolation (► 41). Devoting himself to prayer and study, he wrote in Catalan and Latin on everything from algebra to metaphysics; he is widely seen as the father of the Catalan language. Recalled to the court by Jaume II, he established an Oriental language school at Valldemossa and learnt Arabic with the help of a Moorish slave. He was stoned to death attempting to convert Muslims in Tunisia.

### Junípero Serra
The Mallorcan missionary, Junípero Serra (1713–1784), is honoured in the Capitol in Washington, USA, as 'the founder of California'. Of course California was there already; but it was Serra, sent there at the age of 54 after 14 years in Mexico, who established the missions which grew into some of America's biggest cities, including San Diego and San Francisco. A museum in his home town of Petra (► 51) tells the story. He was beatified in 1988, the first step on the road to sainthood.

### Joan Miró
Though he was not strictly Mallorcan, Joan Miró (1893–1983), the Catalan artist, spent the last 27 years of his life in Mallorca and the islanders have adopted him as their own. His bright, surreal designs adorn everything from tourist posters (the widely used España and Mallorca logos are his) to T-shirts and the mural in the Parc de la Mar in Palma. His house and studio near Palma have been turned into a gallery of his work (► 31).

*Statue of Junípero Serra in Palma*

9

# A Chronology

| | |
|---|---|
| **5000 BC** | Evidence of human habitation in caves on the north coast. |
| **1300–800 BC** | The Talaiotic culture creates settlements like those at Artà and Capocorb Vell. |
| **400 BC** | First references to *honderos* (Balearic slingers) fighting in the Punic Wars. |
| **123 BC** | The island is conquered by the Romans, who name it Balearis Major, introduce vineyards and olives, and establish their capital at Pollentia, now Alcúdia. |
| **AD 426** | Vandal invasion and persecution of Christians. |
| **534** | Byzantine conquest restores Christianity and brings Mallorca into the province of Sardinia. |
| **902** | Arab invasion – Mallorca enters the Caliphate of Córdoba. Oranges and almonds are introduced, along with windmills and irrigation techniques. Palma, known as Medina Mayurqa, is the envy of Europe, with street lights and heated baths. |
| **1229** | The origins of modern Mallorca – conquest by Jaume I of Aragón. Catalan becomes main language. |
| **1275** | Ramón Llull establishes his first hermitage at Puig de Randa. |
| **1276** | On Jaume I's death, his kingdom is divided up and his son Jaume II becomes the first King of Mallorca. |
| **1276–1349** | The 'Golden Age of Independence' – the building of Castell de Bellver, Palau de l'Almudaina and Alcúdia's city walls. |
| **1349** | Jaume III is killed at Llucmajor and the island is reincorporated into Aragón. |
| **1492** | Modern Spain is created with the union of Aragón, Castile and Granada. |

| | |
|---|---|
| **16th–18th centuries** | Repeated pirate attacks lead to the building of watchtowers around the coast. |
| **1715** | After victory in the War of the Spanish Succession, Felipe V imposes central rule and the Castilian language. |
| **1836** | Steamer service opens between Mallorca and Spain. |
| **1879–1898** | Period of 'gold fever' due to the booming export trade in wine and almonds – until the vines are destroyed by the phylloxera virus, leading to mass emigration. |
| **1902–1903** | The Gran Hotel opens in Palma. Thomas Cook runs its first tours to Mallorca. |
| **1936–1939** | The Spanish Civil War, followed by dictatorship under General Franco. |
| **1950** | First charter flight lands in Mallorca. |
| **1960** | Son Sant Joan airport opened. |
| **1966** | Mallorca receives a million tourists. |
| **1975** | Death of Franco; restoration of the monarchy. |
| **1978** | A new constitution grants limited autonomy to the Spanish regions. |
| **1983** | The Balearic Islands become an autonomous region with their capital at Palma. Catalan becomes the official language. |
| **1986** | Spain joins the European Community. |
| **1988** | A new coastal law prohibits further development within 100m of the sea. |
| **1997** | New terminal at Son Sant Joan airport increases capacity to 27 million passengers a year. |
| **2002** | An 'ecotax' on tourists is introduced – and dropped in 2003. |

# Best of Mallorca

*Take the tram to Port de Sóller and the boat to Sa Calobra*

If you only have a short time to visit Mallorca, and are looking for the best way to experience the essence of the island, here are some suggestions for activities and places that shouldn't be missed:

- Spend a day in Palma exploring the old city, then join the evening *passeig* along the waterfront for a drink in one of the island's trendiest bars (➤ 34–38).

- Take the joyride to Sóller on a vintage electric train through the mountains (➤ 46; also ➤ 16).

- Take a boat trip around the coast, and enjoy the view as you pass hidden coves which you cannot reach in a car.

- Walk in the Serra de Tramuntana (➤ 44), breathing in the heady mix of fresh air, sea breeze and scented wild herbs.

- Sit at a quayside restaurant eating fresh fish – choose from any one of the island's ports (➤ 62–69).

- Visit the monastery at Valldemossa where Frédéric Chopin and George Sand spent the winter of 1838–1839 (➤ 48).

- Drive (or walk) to a hilltop sanctuary to experience 'the other Mallorca' – if you really want to get away from it all, stay the night.

- Visit the traditional market at Sineu (➤ 45) to haggle over everything from sausages to sheep.

- Take a trip in a hot-air balloon for stunning views of the whole island (➤ 83).

- Find out where there is a local festival going on (➤ 22) – and drop everything to get there.

# MALLORCA
## how to organise your time

**WALKS AND DRIVES** *14–19*
A Walk Around Palma
A Drive Across the Central Plain
A Day Out by Train and Tram
A Walk from Santa Eugènia
A Drive in the West
The Archduke's Bridlepath

**FINDING PEACE & QUIET** *20–21*

**WHAT'S ON** *22*

# A Walk Around Palma

Start in Plaça d'Espayna by the statue of Jaume I the Conqueror on horseback. With the station behind you, bear left across the square towards Mercat Olivar. Leave via Plaça Olivar and turn left into Carrer Sant Miquel.

Soon you reach Plaça Major with its outdoor cafés and street entertainers. Continue across the square; fork right into Carrer Jaume II.

At the end of this pedestrian shopping street, don't fail to look up at the Moorish-style *modernista* façade of Can Corbella before turning left into Plaça Cort. Beyond a gnarled olive tree you see the town hall. Take the short street to the left of the town hall to reach Plaça Santa Eulàlia; cross this square diagonally and take Carrer Morey.

This brings you into the heart of the old city. Take your time here admiring the courtyards; make sure you don't miss Casa Oleza at No 9. Continue straight on to Carrer Miramar and turn right onto the city walls.

The cathedral (▶ 37) is above you; in order to visit it and the palace, climb the steps up to a large wooden cross. Once back on the walls, continue until you drop to the S'Hort del Rei gardens (▶ 38). Cross Plaça Reina and walk up the Born, turning right by Bar Bosch into Carrer Unió.

Look out for the old Gran Hotel (▶ 36) on your left and the bakery opposite, two good examples of *modernista* style. Beyond the theatre, the road bends left and becomes La Rambla; stroll up this promenade among the flower stalls. At the top of La Rambla, turn right into Carrer Oms and follow it back to Plaça d'Espanya.

## INFORMATION

**Distance** 3.5km
**Time** 2 hours plus coffee, browsing, visits – allow half a day
**Start/end point** Plaça d'Espanya
🍴 Fundació la Caixa (€€)
✉ Plaça Weyler 3

*Plaça Major – a good place to stop for a coffee. There is a craft market held here on summer mornings*

# A Drive Across the Central Plain

This lovely drive criss-crosses the central plain (Es Pla), following old Roman roads through attractive almond and apricot groves and vineyards on its way to a number of small market towns.

Start in Petra by the parish church, following signs to Felanitx. On the way out of the village, you pass the road leading up to Ermita de Bonany (➤ 52).

Keep straight ahead at a roundabout to cross over the C715, the main road from Palma to Manacor. Stay on this country road for 7km, then turn left towards Felanitx. When you see the town ahead of you, take a sharp right turn, signposted to Porreres.

Follow this road across fertile countryside for 12km and into the centre of Porreres.

Leaving Porreres, follow signs to Llucmajor. Stay on this road for 12km as farmland gradually gives way to woods. Reaching Llucmajor, turn left at the roundabout and stay on the ring road to the far end of town, where you turn right, following signs to Algaida.

The road rises and falls for 8km around the foot of Puig de Randa (➤ 41). When you reach Algaida, turn right to briefly join the C715 to Manacor. After 1km, turn left towards Pina and stay on this pretty rural road through Pina and Lloret de Vistalegre, with views of the sierra in the distance as you head towards Sineu (➤ 12, 45).

Just before entering Sineu, turn right to skirt the town centre and turn right again to return to Petra on the old road.

## INFORMATION

**Distance** 81km
**Time** 3 hours
**Start/end point** Petra
🔢 Centre (€)
✉ Avinguda Bisbe Campins, Porreres

*An orchard of almond trees*

# A Day Out by Train and Tram

## INFORMATION

**Time** 1.5 hours each way
**Start point** Plaça d'Espanya
🚌 Most city/island-wide
buses terminate here
**End point** Port de Sóller
🍴 Café Sóller (€)
✉ Plaça Constitució, Sóller
☎ 971 630010

The opening of a railway line from Palma to Sóller in 1912, and a tram linking Sóller to its port the following year, brought the northwest coast within easy reach of the capital. The vintage carriages are still in use, providing a joyride for tourists and a relief for locals from the terrors of the Palma–Sóller road. Five trains a day leave from Plaça d'Espanya in Palma – the 10.50 is labelled the *turístico* but all you get for the extra cost is a more crowded train and a short photo stop.

The train, all mahogany panels and brass fittings, leaves Palma amid a bustle of hisses, hoots and whistles before rattling down the city streets and into the suburbs. Soon you are out on the plain, passing small country stations and pigs rooting beneath the trees. You can get off at Bunyola and climb up the hill to reach the centre of this sleepy village, with cafés on the main square.

*Take the miniature train from Palma to Sóller*

Stay on the train and soon you start to climb, entering a 3km tunnel before returning to daylight for the drop, through a dizzying series of bends, to Sóller (➤ 46).

The 'Orange Express' tram to Port de Sóller runs hourly, connecting with the arrival of the train. Stand on the platform as it clatters through orchards and back gardens and you can imagine you are living 50 years earlier. The 5km journey to the port takes 20 minutes.

If you do not want to return the same way, there are regular express buses returning to Palma via the Sóller tunnel.

# A Walk from Santa Eugènia

This simple walk gives spectacular views for the minimum of effort. Leave the village of Santa Eugènia and head in the direction of Santa Maria del Camí. After 1km turn left to Ses Coves along a narrow lane which bends left, then descends and you see Ses Coves ('the caves') used at various times as pirate hideaways and wine cellars. One cave contains an ancient wine-press. When the road divides, fork left; soon you reach some iron gates at the entrance to a track on your right.

*Selling olives at Santa Maria del Camí market*

Here you have an optional detour to the summit of Puig d'En Marron, adding an hour to your walk. Step over the low wall besides the gates and climb until the road runs out. Continue along a mud track through the pine woods, keeping right at each fork, until you emerge onto a wide open plateau. Return to the iron gates by the same route and turn right to rejoin the main walk.

Follow the lane briefly uphill; when the lane divides, take the track on the left. After passing an arched entrance to a well, turn immediately left through an orchard towards a house.

To the right of the house, the wall is marked with a red dot; climb from here to a pass. Here you can clamber over a stone wall to your left to reach the cross on the summit of Puig de Santa Eugènia. This is the high point of the walk, with wonderful views that stretch across the plain to the mountains in the distance. On the opposite clifftop is one of Mallorca's oddest sights – the cockpit of a broken-up plane.

Retrace your steps to the stone wall and then follow the path that leads through the bushes on your left to return to Santa Eugènia.

## INFORMATION

**Distance** 4.5km (optional detour adds 3km)
**Time** 1–2 hours
**Start/end point** Santa Eugènia
🚌 From Palma to Santa Maria del Camí with connecting bus at Santa Eugènia
🍴 Ca Na Cantona (€)
✉ Carrer Balenguera, Santa Eugènia
☎ 971 144031

# A Drive in the West

This drive gives an excellent introduction to the mountain and coastal scenery of western Mallorca.

## INFORMATION

**Distance** 62km
**Time** 3 hours plus lunch and time at La Granja
**Start/end point** Andratx
🍴 La Granja (€)
✉ 971 610032

Start in Andratx, taking the C710 to Estellencs about halfway up the main street. Immediately the road begins to climb through pine woods and tunnels, with occasional glimpses of the sea. Follow this beautiful twisting coast road to the village of Estellencs, one of the prettiest in Mallorca, with its ochre-coloured houses, narrow, steep cobbled streets and women doing their washing at the village well. After another 5km, stop at the Mirador de Ses Animes and clamber up to the 16th-century watchtower for views right along the northwest coast. Soon after this you reach Banyalbufar (➤ 58), with its spectacular terracing.

When the C710 turns off left towards Valldemossa, keep straight on the PM110, signposted to Palma. After 1km you see a sign to La Granja on your right. You could easily spend 2–3 hours at this display of Mallorcan traditions (➤ 32).

Leaving La Granja, take the narrow road to Puigpunyent from the car park. Follow this road for 10km, a dramatic journey through olive groves in the shadow of Puig de Galatzó. The road continues through Puigpunyent and on to Galilea (➤ 50), a mountain village with a couple of tapas bars and views out to sea. From here the road twists and turns down to the village of Es Capdella. Turn right in the village and follow signs back to Andratx.

*You pass several coastal watchtowers, including this one near the village of Estellencs*

# The Archduke's Bridlepath Walk

This walk was mapped out by Archduke Ludwig Salvator during tours of his estates by mule; as well as spectacular coastal views, it gives an introduction to traditional mountain industries. You pass *sitjas* (round charcoal ovens), *casas de neu* (snow pits where winter snows were stored beneath a layer of ash), *forns de calç* (lime kilns) and *caças a coll* (thrush nets slung between the trees). The route is for experienced walkers only. Take food and water, a map, compass and whistle and protection from sun, wind and rain. The weather on the mountains can change very quickly.

Begin at the car park opposite Bar Sa Mata on the road through Valldemossa. Climb the hill behind the car park towards the cemetery. Take the second right (Carrer Joan Fuster), then first left (Carrer de les Oliveres), continuing onto a rough track when the road runs out. You climb gently at first, towards a group of pines, then more steeply, following red waymarks to a clearing. From here it is a short, tough climb to a mirador and the start of the Camí de S'Arxiduc, marked by a ruined stone refuge.

Follow the waymarks onto a high plateau and continue for about two hours. For the best views of all, a one-hour diversion (just as the main path bears round to the right for its descent) takes you to the summit of the Teix, from where most of Mallorca is visible on a clear day. The path drops back down to Valldemossa through a wooded valley, passing a shelter where you can camp in summer.

For a shorter walk to the foot of the Teix, you can simply do the final section in reverse. From Valldemossa walk past Son Gual, the large old house with a tower seen just above the main road as you enter Palma. Turn left after 10 minutes onto a wide track (signed 'Refugi'). The climb through the valley to the shelter and back will take a couple of hours if you walk briskly.

## INFORMATION

**Distance** 13km
**Time** 6 hours
**Start/end point** Valldemossa
🚌 From Palma, Deià or Port de Sóller
🍴 Take a picnic

*There are splendid views of the coastline from the Archduke's estates*

19

# Finding Peace & Quiet

**RIGHTS OF WAY**

Walkers have the right of way on all coastal paths, plus routes to miradors, monasteries and mountain peaks (except Puig Major). In recent years, many landowners have attempted to deny access by erecting 'private' signs. If challenged, just state clearly where you are going.

*Almond trees near Andratx – it is still surprisingly easy to get away from it all in Mallorca*

If you want peace and quiet in Mallorca, go in winter – only 10 per cent of foreign tourists visit between November and March. The island is particularly beautiful in February, when almond blossom carpets the ground like snow. Even in the height of summer, there are plenty of opportunities to escape the crowds. Half of the locals live in Palma, and 90 per cent of the tourists stay on a few small stretches of coast – which leaves large areas of Mallorca just waiting to be explored.

## WALKING

The obvious areas are the mountains, especially the Serra de Tramuntana (▶ 44). At the lower levels, up to around 700m, you walk through *garrigue*, a typical Mediterranean landscape where Aleppo pines mix with wild olives and the stony ground sprouts beautiful wild flowers – orchids and peonies and cistus and asphodel – in spring. (Spring here arrives early, from late February through to May.) Higher up, you reach the *maquis* scrubland, where little grows apart from thorny bushes of heather, bracken, rosemary and broom. Above 1,000m the land is barren – but the views from this height are magnificent and the sense of isolation complete.

*The wetlands of S'Albufera are a protected reserve*

Take sensible precautions when walking in the mountains – good boots, extra clothing, food and water, a map, compass and whistle. If you prefer more gentle walks, just strike out along any of the minor roads between the small towns on the plain, or follow a coastal footpath to find your own private bay.

## BIRDS

Mallorca is a paradise for birdwatchers, who come from all over Europe each spring and autumn to see migrating birds on their way to and from wintering in Africa. The best times are April to May and September to October, and the best areas are S'Albufera (► 42) and the Salines de Llevant near Ses Salines. The reedbeds of S'Albufera come alive each spring with the song of herons and warblers; other species include egrets, terns, hoopoes, sandpipers and woodchat shrike. Numerous wading birds and wildfowl are attracted to the salt marshes at Ses Salines, including plovers, stilts, water rails and black-tailed godwits. Good spots for watching seabirds include Cap de Ses Salines on the south coast and Cap de Formentor in the northeast (► 27), where shags and shearwaters nestle on the cliffs.

### BIRDS OF PREY

The mountains of the Serra de Tramuntana are a haven for birds of prey, including ospreys, peregrines, Montagu's harriers and Eleanora's falcons. Rarest of all are the black vultures, of which only a few dozen remain in the area around Lluc monastery. An exhibition at the monastery describes a conservation programme to protect both these and another endangered species, the Mallorcan midwife toad. The best places to see black vultures, and other predatory birds, are at the Cúber and Gorg Blau reservoirs on the road through the mountains from Lluc to Sóller.

21

# What's On

| | |
|---|---|
| **JANUARY** | *Cabalgata de los Reyes Magos* (5 Jan): The Three Kings arrive by boat in Palma to distribute gifts to the city's children.<br>*Sant Antoni Abat* (16–17 Jan): Processions of pets and farm animals: Palma, Artà, Sa Pobla.<br>*Sant Sebastià* (19 Jan): Bonfires and barbecues in Palma's squares. |
| **FEBRUARY** | *Sa Rúa* (final weekend before Lent): Carnival in Palma and elsewhere with bonfires, fancy dress and processions of decorated floats. In Montuïri the Carnival is known as *Els Darres Dies (the last days)*. |
| **MARCH/APRIL** | *Semana Santa* (Holy Week): Easter preparation begins on Palm Sunday, with the blessing of palm and olive branches. During Holy Week the biggest Palma procession is on Maundy Thursday. On the evening of Good Friday a figure of Christ is lowered from his cross in Pollença and carried down the Calvary steps in silence. A similar event takes place in Felanitx. |
| **MAY** | *Moros i Cristians* (8–10 May): Mock battles between heroes and infidels in Sóller, commemorating 1561 when local women helped to defeat a band of Turkish pirates. |
| **JUNE** | *Sant Pere* (28–29 Jun): Processions of boats in Palma, Port d'Andratx and Port d'Alcúdia in honour of the patron saint of fishermen. |
| **JULY** | *La Verge del Carme* (16 Jul): Boat processions in ports including Cala Rajada, Port de Pollença and Port de Sóller.<br>*Santa Catalina Thomás* (27–28 Jul): Homage to Mallorca's patron saint in Valldemossa. |
| **AUGUST** | *Sant Bartomeu* (24 Aug): Devil-dancing in Montuïri at one of Mallorca's oldest festivals.<br>*Sant Agustí* (28 Aug): *Cavallets* dances in Felanitx, with children dressed up as cardboard horses being chased by giants to the accompaniment of bagpipes, flutes and drums. |
| **SEPTEMBER/OCTOBER** | Harvest festivals including a melon festival in Vilafranca de Bonany (second Sun in Sep), a wine fair in Binissalem (last Sun in Sep), and a *botifarró* (blood sausage) festival in Sant Joan (third Sun in Oct). |
| **DECEMBER** | *Festa de l'Estendard* (31 Dec): Anniversary of the Christian conquest; procession from Palma's town hall to Mass at the cathedral. |

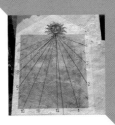

# MALLORCA's
## top 25 sights

The sights are shown on the maps on the inside front cover and inside back cover, numbered **1**–**25** alphabetically

**1** Alcúdia *24*

**2** Artà *25*

**3** Badia de Palma (Palma Bay) *26*

**4** Cap de Formentor *27*

**5** Castell d'Alaró *28*

**6** Coves d'Artà *29*

**7** Deià *30*

**8** Fundació Pilar i Joan Miró *31*

**9** La Granja *32*

**10** Lluc *33*

**11** Palma *34*

**12** Palma's Castell de Bellver *35*

**13** Palma's Fundació la Caixa *36*

**14** Palma's La Seu *37*

**15** Palma's Palau de l'Almudaina *38*

**16** Pollença *39*

**17** Port de Pollença *40*

**18** Puig de Randa *41*

**19** S'Albufera *42*

**20** Sa Calobra *43*

**21** Serra de Tramuntana *44*

**22** Sineu *45*

**23** Sóller *46*

**24** Son Marroig *47*

**25** Valldemossa *48*

23

# Alcúdia

**This is a gem of a place. It is a perfectly restored walled city on the site of a Roman settlement, with remains of Roman houses and an amphitheatre. You see a maze of narrow streets enclosed by medieval ramparts, presented as a model of Mallorca's new tourist image.**

There were Phoenician and Greek settlements, but Alcúdia's heyday was in the 2nd century BC, when as Pollentia ('power') it was the capital of Roman Mallorca. Destroyed in the 6th century by Vandals, the town returned to greatness under the Moors, who built *al-kudia* ('the town on the hill'). The existing walls were added after the Spanish conquest in the 14th century.

*Portal del Moll, once the gateway to Alcúdia from its port, leads directly into the heart of the city*

You enter the city through one of the two town gates – the Portal del Moll, with two square towers and two palm trees standing guard, is the symbol of Alcúdia. The narrow streets of the old town, especially Carrer d'en Serra, are redolent of Palma's Arab quarter. A short walk from the parish church of Sant Jaume takes you to three interesting sights, connected by signposted footpaths. Closest are the remains of Roman houses at Pollentia, **Ciutat Romà**; near here are the well-preserved Teatre Romà (Roman amphitheatre), and Oratori de Santa Anna, one of the islands's oldest churches. Explore the Roman remains, then interpret them at the **Museu Monogràfic de Pollentia**.

# Artà

**Derived from the Arabic word *jertan* ('garden'), Artà has been occupied for at least 3,000 years, as evidenced by the Bronze Age site at Ses Països, just outside the town. Nowadays Artà is a prosperous little town near the coast, which gets particularly lively each Tuesday on market day.**

From the parish church of Transfiguració del Senyor, an avenue of cypress trees leads to Artà's crowning glory, its hilltop fortress and Santuari de Sant Salvador. The view down over the rooftops, a jumble of tiles in every shade of brown, is one of the sights of Mallorca. On the site of a Moorish fortress, the original sanctuary walls and chapel were rebuilt in the 19th century. Walk around the battlements, rest in a courtyard, then look into the church with its vivid paintings of two Mallorcan heroes – Jaume the Conqueror receiving the surrender of the *walis*, and Ramón Llull being stoned to death in Tunisia. There is also a painting of Sant Antoni, patron saint of Artà and of animals, seen as always with a small pig. Each January the saint is commemorated with a masked procession and a blessing of pets. Artà's big festival, Sant Antoni de Juny, dates back to 1581 and features dancers with cardboard horses strapped to their hips.

The coastline north of Artà contains some of Mallorca's wildest and beautiful beaches, including the cove of Cala Torta.

**INFORMATION**

➕ E2

🚌 From Palma and Cala Rajada

❓ Market held Tue; Sant Antoni Abat, procession and blessing of pets, 16–17 Jan; Sant Antoni de Juny, *cavallets* horse dances, 13 Jun

*A flight of steps leads to Artà's hilltop sanctuary*

25

# Badia de Palma (Palma Bay)

## INFORMATION

➕ B3

🍴 Numerous bars and restaurants in all the resorts (€)

🚌 From Palma to all the resorts

🚢 Boat tours of Palma Bay in summer from Palma, S'Arenal, Palma Nova and Magaluf

♿ Level beach promenades at Platja de Palma and Magaluf

🔁 Castell de Bellver (▶ 35)

**The good, the bad and the ugly sides of Mallorca's tourist development meet along this 25km stretch of coast. Like it or loathe it, you are bound to spend some time in Palma Bay.**

The former villages of S'Arenal and Magaluf sit facing each other across Palma Bay. Once, a fisherman casting his net at S'Arenal could have gazed around an empty coastline where the only prominent buildings would have been Palma's cathedral and castle. Nowadays he would barely be able to distinguish them among a continuous stretch of hotels, a concrete jungle extending all the way to Magaluf. And he wouldn't be there anyway as there are few fish left to catch.

Even if you are not staying here, you should visit at least once to see some of the best, and the worst, that Mallorca has to offer. Each of the resorts has its own character – young or old, British or German, cheap-and-cheerful or jet-set rich. One moment you can be in Portals Nous, its marina crammed with millionaires' yachts (you have to be seriously rich just to look at the restaurant menus), the next in seedy Magaluf, all British pubs and wet T-shirt contests.

Occasionally you come across a glimpse of what this coastline must have been like. Follow the road beyond Magaluf through the pine woods. Suddenly you are among tiny coves where, out of season, you might still find your own private beach. Eventually you reach the headland of Cap de Cala Figuera (▶ 50) where you can look back at sweeping views of the bay. Cliffs plunge into the clear blue sea, with not a hotel in sight. Come up here at midnight for utter peace and solitude; even so, if you listen carefully you might just be able to hear the disco beat of Magaluf pounding away beneath you.

## Cap de Formentor

**This wild peninsula on Mallorca's northeast tip has stunning views, sandy beaches and the island's original luxury hotel. Hotel Formentor has been pampering the rich and famous ever since it opened in 1929.**

The 20km drive from Port de Pollença to Mallorca's most northerly point has dramatic scenery. Cliffs 400m tall jut into the sea, their weird rock formations attracting nesting seabirds, while pine trees seem to grow out of the rocks. The drive is famously scary – local legend has it that the parish priest and bus driver arrived at the Pearly Gates, and only the driver was admitted The reason? He had led far more people to pray.

Six kilometres from Port de Pollença you reach the Mirador des Colomer – scramble up

the steps for views over a rocky islet. A path opposite leads to an old watchtower from which you can see the whole of the peninsula as well as the bays of Pollença and Alcúdia. The road continues through pine woods and past more *miradors* (each one indicated with a picture of a camera) before tunnelling through En Fumat mountain, where you look down over Mallorca's most inaccessible beach. Eventually you reach a lighthouse with the inevitable bar and shop, with views all the way to Menorca on a good day.

On the way back, stop at Formentor beach and the Hotel Formentor. The fine sandy beach used to be reserved for the hotel's guests, but democracy has opened it to the masses.

### INFORMATION

- E1
- Café with snacks at Cap de Formentor (€); restaurant (€€€) in Hotel Formentor
- From Palma and Port de Pollença in summer
- From Port de Pollença to Formentor beach and Cap de Formentor in summer
- The best time to see birds and flowers is spring

*Walkers on the path to the viewpoint at Mirador des Colomar*

27

## Castell d'Alaró

### INFORMATION

🔹 C2
🔹 Sanctuary: 971 182112
🔹 Open access
🔹 Es Verger (€€) on the way up; simple restaurant (€€) at the sanctuary
🔹 From Palma to Alaró
🔹 Orient (▶ 51)

**A popular walk, ending with a steep climb, to a ruined castle and hilltop chapel offering spectacular views all the way to the sea.**

A castle has stood on this site since Moorish times; it was so impregnable that the Arab commander was able to hold out for two years after the Christian conquest. Later, in 1285, two heroes of Mallorcan independence, Cabrit and Brassa, defended the castle against Alfonsó III of Aragón and were burned alive on a spit when he finally took it by storm. Their punishment was a consequence of their impudent defiance of the king. They pretended to confuse Alfonsó's name with that of a local fish – *anfós*, shouting: 'We like our *anfós* grilled.' The present ruins date from the 15th century and seem almost to grow out of the rock, dominating the landscape for miles around.

The climb up here is one of Mallorca's most popular walks, especially on Sundays. From the town of Alaró it is a stiff climb of about two hours, following the signs from the PM210 to Orient; you can also leave from Orient (▶ 51), following a small path opposite L'Hermitage hotel, again taking around two hours in total. The paths converge above Es Verger restaurant (you can even bring a car this far if you don't mind the potholes and the hairpin bends), where you can fill up with roast lamb to fortify you for the final steep section.

*The view from inside the ruins at Castell d'Alaró*

At last you reach the castle, 800m above sea level; look back at the view, stretching across the entire plain to Palma and out to sea. A few minutes further brings you to the summit, with a small chapel and sanctuary, and (bliss!) a restaurant and bar. You can stay the night here in one of the simple rooms.

# Coves d'Artà

**A fascinating network of underground caverns, whose weird stalactites and stalagmites conjure up mysterious images of Heaven and Hell.**

If you only have time to visit one set of caves on the east coast, this is the one to see. Now that they are a sanitised tourist attraction, it is hard to imagine how French geologist Édouard Martel felt when he first stepped into these caves, dark, mysterious and terrifying, in 1876. In fact they had been known about for centuries – Jaume I found 2,000 Arabs hiding here with their cattle during the Christian conquest and they were later used by hermits, pirates and smugglers – but it was Martel who first studied and chronicled these grottoes, 46m above the sea at Cap Vermell, at the instigation of Archduke Ludwig Salvator. Another early visitor was Jules Verne; the caves are said to have inspired his *Journey to the Centre of the Earth*.

The guided tour comes with special effects and the various chambers are given Dantesque names – Hell, Purgatory, Paradise. The descent into Hell is swiftly followed by a *son et lumière* display. Stalactites point down from the mouldy roof like daggers, somehow defying gravity. One of the chambers is as large as the nave of Palma cathedral, and the Queen of Pillars, a stalagmite 22m tall, could almost be a Gothic column. It is growing upwards at the rate of 2cm every 100 years; in another 5,000 years or so it will be joined to the ceiling.

You emerge from the caves to a view of the sea, framed by the cavern entrance. Disabled visitors and others with limited mobility will find the staircases in here particularly difficult. All visitors should be sensibly shod, as the floor can be slippery.

## INFORMATION

- ✚ F2
- ☎ 971 841293
- 🕐 Jul–Sep, daily 10–7; Oct–Jun, daily 10–5
- 🍴 Bars at Platja de Canyamel near by (€)
- 🚌 From Artà and Cala Rajada in summer
- ♿ None
- 💷 Expensive
- ↔ Artá (► 25)

*Artificial lighting results in some spectacular colours in the caves*

# Deià

## Deià

**INFORMATION**

➕ B2
🍴 Wide choice of restaurants and bars (€–€€€)
🚌 From Palma, Valldemossa and Port de Sóller
↔ Son Marroig (➤ 47)
❓ Classical music festival, Aug–Sep

*Cars parked in the main square at Deià, popular with artists*

**This idyllic village of green-shuttered, ochre-coloured houses has become a millionaires' hideaway in the shadow of the Teix mountain.**

Deià could have been just another pretty Mallorcan village had Robert Graves not decided to make it his home. The English poet and novelist first moved here in 1932 with his mistress Laura Riding and returned in 1946 with his second wife. Muses followed, friends came to stay, and before long Deià had established a reputation as a foreign artists' colony. Now it is on every tourist itinerary as the prime example of 'the other Mallorca', and this small village contains two luxury hotels. Rich foreign residents, like the actor Michael Douglas, are

apt to bemoan the arrival of tour buses; the few locals who remain are philosophical about outsiders.

Graves was hardly the first to discover Deià. An 1878 guidebook noted its 'collection of strange and eccentric foreigners' and it has stayed that way ever since. Climb the Carrer es Puig, Deià's only real street, passing ceramic Stations of the Cross, to reach the parish church and the small cemetery where Graves is buried. His tombstone, like many others, is inscribed in simple handwriting set into the drying concrete – Robert Graves, Poeta, 1895–1985. Graves' house, Ca n'Alluny, has recently been acquired by the government and it's expected to open in 2005.

From Deià you can scramble down to Cala de Deià, a small shingle beach set in an attractive cove, where local artists still continue the Graves tradition of naked swimming and long parties at weekends.

# Fundació Pilar i Joan Miró

**Joan Miró's house and studio were built on a hillside to capitalise on the special quality of the Mallorcan light, which was so important to him.**

The painter and sculptor Joan Miró spent most of his life in Barcelona, but both his wife and mother were Mallorcan and he always longed to return to the scene of his childhood holidays to draw inspiration from what he called 'the light of Mallorca'. In 1956, aged 63, he bought a house and studio in Cala Major. He lived here until he died in 1983, after which the building was enlarged to hold a permanent exhibition of his works. Changing displays of Miró's work are shown in galleries of bleached stone.

The collection includes more than 100 paintings, 25 sculptures and 3,000 studio pieces but only a small amount is displayed at any one time. The paintings are almost childish, all vivid splashes of bright primary colours, influenced by his love of peasant traditions and his fascination with *siurells* (clay whistles). Anyone tempted to remark that their child could do better should take a look at the heavily realistic work that Miró was producing aged eight – the fantasy came later. Works on display include the draft for UNESCO's *Mural del Sol* in Paris.

Glance into Miró's studio, left untouched since his death, with work in progress, open tins of paint and black stains all over the floor.

## INFORMATION

 B2

✉ Carrer Joan de Saridakis 29, Cala Major

☎ 971 701420

🕐 15 May–15 Sep, Tue–Sat 10–7, Sun 10–3; 16 Sep–14 May, Tue–Sat 10–6, Sun 10–3

🍴 Café (€)

🚌 6 from Palma

♿ Good

Ⓜ Moderate

*A sculpture by Joan Miró in the grounds of his former studio*

31

# La Granja

## INFORMATION

✚ B2

✉ Carretera Esporles –
Puigpunyent, km2,
Esporles

☎ 971 610032;
www.lagranja.net

◷ Apr–Sep, daily 10–7;
Oct–Mar, daily 10–6

🍴 Restaurant (€)

🚌 From Palma

♿ None

💷 Expensive

↔ Banyalbufar (▶ 58)

❓ Folk fiesta Wed, Fri
3.30–5

**This grand house, standing on a site occupied since Moorish times, was once a Cistercian monastery, and now provides a fascinating insight into Mallorcan life in earlier days.**

This country house, just south of Banyalbufar, is on a site known since Roman times for its natural spring. When Jaume I conquered Mallorca he divided the island into four feudal estates, giving one to Count Nuno Sanç, who settled at La Granja. In 1239 the Count handed the estate to Cistercian monks to found Mallorca's first monastery. Since 1447 it has been a private house owned by various noble families; most of what you see today dates from the 17th century.

Highlights of the tour include an aristocratic drawing-room with its own theatre, the family chapel and a dungeon with a torture chamber – but the real reason for visiting La Granja is to learn about rural Mallorcan traditions. Workshops, cellars and kitchens contain displays of everyday objects. And on Wednesday and Friday afternoons, women in traditional costume give demonstrations of lace-making, embroidery and spinning, donkeys turn threshing-wheels and there are tastings of cheese, wine, sausages, doughnuts and fig cake. Escape from the tour groups by walking in the grounds, which contain botanical gardens, waterfalls and a thousand-year-old yew – there is a 1,200m signed walk. La Granja is still a working farm and you may see pigs, turkeys, chickens and goats as well as displays of agricultural implements and tools.

If you have not gorged yourself on free samples during the course of your visit, the restaurant serves good Mallorcan staple dishes like *pa amb oli* and *sopes mallorquines*.

## Lluc

**This is Mallorca's most sacred site – a former monastery in a spectacular setting in the Serra de Tramuntana, housing a much-venerated ancient wooden statue of the Virgin.**

Lluc has been a centre of pilgrimage since the 13th century when an Arab shepherd boy, newly converted to Christianity, discovered a dark wooden statue of the Virgin in a cleft in the rock. The image was placed in the local church but three times it returned miraculously to its cave, whereupon the villagers recognised a message from God and built a chapel to house it.

*La Moreneta* ('the Little Dark One') is now encrusted with precious stones, and sits in a chapel decorated with the arms of every Mallorcan town. Pilgrims and tourists queue to pay homage, especially on Sundays at 11AM before the daily concerts by Els Blauets choir. The choir, named after their blue cassocks, was established in 1531, comprising 40 boys, 'natives of Mallorca, of pure blood, sound in grammar and song'. The service is marred by the whirring and flashing of cameras, and if it's meditation you seek, come back instead for the evening Mass.

The monastery complex includes Els Porxets, the former pilgrims' quarters with stabling beneath the rooms, and the Way of the Rosary, with touches by Antoni Gaudí. From the hilltop cross you look down over a farmland valley and up into the pine-covered mountains. You can stay at Lluc but it is more like a hotel than a hermitage – the 100 'cells' have en suite bathrooms and there are restaurants and bars. There is also a museum – in addition to the displays of ceramics, chalices and coins there is a collection of paintings by the 20th-century Mallorcan artist Josep Coll Bardolet.

### INFORMATION

- ✚ C1
- ☎ 971 871525
- ◷ Museum: daily 10–1.30, 2.30–5.15; Monastery: daily 9–8.30
- ☎ Sa Fonda (€€) in the former monks' refectory
- ◲ Two buses daily from Palma and Inca
- ◴ Monastery: free. Museum: cheap
- ◰ Sa Calobra (➤ 43), Serra de Tramuntana (➤ 44)
- ◲ Choir concert daily at 11.15 during Mass; second service at dusk open to those staying overnight; annual night-time pilgrimage from Palma to Lluc on foot (48km) – usually held in first week of Aug

## Palma

### INFORMATION

✚ B2

ℹ Plaça de la Reina 2
  ☎ 971 712 216;
  Ca'n Solleric, Passeig des
  Born 27
  ☎ 971 724090;
  Parc de les Estacions
  ☎ 971 754329

🍴 Wide range of cafés and
  restaurants (€–€€€)

❓ Festivals throughout the
  year, including daily
  processions during Holy
  Week and fishing boat
  procession (Festival of
  Sant Pere) in June

**Palma comes as a surprise to many people: stylish, sophisticated, intimate yet bursting with life. Half of Mallorca's population live here, enjoying the island's best restaurants and shops as well as a thriving arts scene.**

Known to the Arabs as Medina Mayurqa and to Mallorcans simply as *Ciutat* (City), Palma is named after the Roman city of Palmaria. Here you can uncover the different layers of Mallorcan history. The Roman city still exists, a metre or two beneath the ground; Roman remains are still discovered near the cathedral, itself built on the site of a mosque that was once a Roman temple. The royal palace replaced an Arab *alcázar*.

The city you see today, however, is a relatively recent creation. The tree-lined promenades of La Rambla and Passeig des Born, home to florists and newspaper sellers, were built in the 19th century on a dried-up river bed. The walls which once surrounded the city were pulled down to create the ring road Las Avingudas, and Passeig Marítim, the waterfront highway and promenade, was only reclaimed from the sea in the 1950s.

Most of the main sights are located within the area bounded by the old walls, especially to the north and east of the cathedral. Wander along any alley in the ancient Arab quarter, peering through wrought-iron gates and heavy wooden doors, and you will be rewarded with glimpses of one magnificent patio after another, with their stone staircases, galleries and arcades.

But you have not truly seen Palma until you have surveyed it from the waterfront, with the cathedral and Almudaina palace rising proudly above the defensive walls of the old city, their golden sandstone lit up by the afternoon sun.

# Palma's Castell de Bellver

**A well-preserved 14th-century royal fortress with fragrant pine woods, an interesting museum and superb views over Palma Bay. Castell de Bellver is unique among Spanish castles in being entirely round.**

## INFORMATION

✚ B2

✉ Carrer Camilo José Cela s/n, Parc Bellver

☎ 971 730657

🕐 Apr–Sep, Mon–Sat 8am–8.30pm, Sun 10–7; Oct–Mar, Mon–Sat 8–7.15, Sun 10–5

🚌 3 or 6 to Plaça Gomila

💶 Cheap; free Sun

Looking up at this castle, so perfectly maintained, it is hard to believe that it has been standing for almost 700 years. It was begun by Jaume II in 1300 and built by Pere Salvà, architect of the Almudaina Palace. Three large towers surround a central courtyard, connected by an arch to a free-standing keep. The courtyard itself is on two levels,

*Looking down on the circular courtyard of Bellver Castle*

the ground floor with semicircular arches and a flat roof, the upper level with Gothic arches and rib-vaulting. For the full effect, walk around the moat then climb onto the roof and look down into the courtyard to compare the contrasting styles. While you are there, look out over the city and the bay for one of the best views in Palma (Bellver means 'lovely view' in Catalan).

For many centuries the castle was used as a prison; Jaume III's widow and sons were incarcerated here for most of their lives. These days it contains Palma's museum of municipal history which traces the development of the city through its artefacts, with pottery from Talaiotic, Roman, Arab and Spanish periods.

You can get there by car or taxi, or by bus to Plaça Gomila, climbing through the woods above Carrer de Bellver.

# Palma's Fundació la Caixa

## INFORMATION

✚ B2
✉ Plaça Weyler 3
☎ 971 178500
🕐 Tue–Sat 10–9, Sun 10–2
🍴 Café and restaurant (€€)
♿ Good
▨ Free

**A quality hotel in the *modernista* style, dating from the turn of the 20th century, has been lovingly restored and is now an art gallery.**

The Gran Hotel was Palma's first luxury hotel when it opened in 1903. Designed by the Catalan architect Lluís Domènech i Montaner, it was the building that began the craze for *modernista* (art nouveau) architecture in the city. Restored by the Fundació la Caixa and reopened in 1993, the art gallery has changing exhibitions and a permanent display of paintings by Hermen Anglada-Camarasa, the founder of the 'Pollença school'. On the ground floor there is a bookshop and a trendy café-bar.

*Artistry can be admired inside and out at Fundació la Caixa – the 'in' place to meet for coffee and cakes*

# Palma's La Seu

**The glory of Palma – a magnificent Gothic cathedral whose sandstone walls and flying buttresses seem to rise out of the sea.**

Anything you see inside Palma cathedral will come as a disappointment once you have stood on the seafront and gazed up at its golden sandstone exterior, climbing above the old city walls. La Seu stands out utterly from its surroundings, a demonstration of the might of Mallorca's Christian conquerors to all who arrived by sea. Tradition has it that a storm arose as Jaume I was sailing towards Mallorca. He vowed that if he landed safely he would build a great church in honour of the Virgin. On New Year's Day 1230, a day after the fall of Palma, the foundation stone was symbolically laid on the site of the city's main mosque. Work continued for 400 years – and had to be resumed in 1851 when an earthquake destroyed the west front. More touches were added by the Catalan architect Antoni Gaudí.

You enter through a side door, passing a small museum; head for the west portal and gaze down the long nave. Light pours in through one of the world's largest rose windows, 12m across and studded with 1,236 pieces of stained glass. The columns are ringed with wrought-iron candelabra by Gaudí; his most controversial addition is the unfinished *Crown of Thorns*, fashioned from cardboard and cork and suspended above the altar. Be sure to walk around to the south front, facing the sea, to look at the Portal del Mirador, a 15th-century door by Guillem Sagrera featuring scenes from the Last Supper.

## INFORMATION

- B2
- Plaça d'Almoina
- 971 723130
- Jun–Sep, Mon–Fri 10–6.15, Sat 10–2.15; Apr–May & Oct, Mon–Fri 10-–5.15, Sat 10–2.15; Nov–Mar, Mon–Fri 10–3.15, Sat 10–2.15
- Few
- Moderate (free for services)
- High Mass, Sun 10.30

*A statue in a niche on the façade of the cathedral*

## Palma's Palau de l'Almudaina

### INFORMATION

➕ B2

✉ Carrer Palau Reial

☎ 971 214134

🕐 Palace: Apr–Sep, Mon–Fri
10–6.30, Sat 10–2;
Oct–Mar, Mon–Fri 10–2,
4–6, Sat 10–2
Gardens: open access

♿ Wheelchair access on
request

🎟 Palace: moderate
Gardens: free

❓ Still used by King Juan
Carlos for official
functions in Palma

**The imposing palace of Almudaina (meaning 'citadel') was once the residence of the kings of Mallorca, and is still used by today's Spanish royal family.**

A royal palace has stood here since the Muslim *walis* (governors) built their *alcázar* (fortress) after the Arab conquest. It was converted into Gothic style under Jaume II, but elements of Islamic architecture remain – like the Moorish arches seen from the seafront, lit up at night like a row of lanterns. The courtyard, laid out in 1309 and flanked by palm trees, is seen at its best in late afternoon when the sun falls on the cathedral towers. Off the courtyard is the royal chapel, Capella de Santa Ana.

The S'Hort del Rei gardens beneath the palace make a pleasant spot to sit and from here you can watch the world go by. Look for the Arc de la Drassana, once the gateway to the royal docks; near by is a statue of a *hondero* or Balearic slinger. The gardens were rebuilt in the 1960s and their best-known landmark is Joan Miró's *Egg* sculpture, which few people can resist sticking their heads through.

*The Islamic style of Palma's royal palace reflects its origins as a Muslim fortress*

# Pollença

**The attractions of Pollença have long been a magnet for tourists, but the town has learned to accept and adapt to tourism while still preserving its individuality.**

Located at the eastern end of the Serra de Tramuntana and tucked between two hills, each topped by a sacred site, Pollença is the perfect Mallorcan town. Large enough to avoid being twee but small enough to wander round in a morning, it has none of the feel of other towns that have succumbed under the sheer weight of tourism. Café life is still the rule; if you want to join in, come on a Sunday morning when the Plaça Major is filled with market stalls and, after church, the locals congregate to relax in the nearby Café Espanyol.

The Pont Romà (Roman bridge) on the edge of town is a clue to Pollença's long history. The name Pollença dates from the 14th century, when settlers from Alcúdia named the town after their former Roman capital. From the former Jesuit convent, now the town hall, you climb 365 steps, lined with cypress trees, to the Calvari church, with its ancient wooden cross and views of Puig de Maria. The church steps are the scene of a moving procession each Good Friday, when a figure of Christ is taken down from a cross and carried down the steps by torchlight.

The **Municipal Museum** in the former Dominican convent contains the remains of prehistoric sculptures shaped like bulls, as well as a *mandala* (Tibetan sand painting) given by the Dalai Lama in 1990. The cloisters of the convent are the venue for Pollença's celebrated classical music festival.

## INFORMATION

⊞ D1
🍴 Cafés and restaurants (€€)
🚌 From Palma
❓ Market Sun; classical music festival, Jul–Sep; *Devallement* procession, Good Fri; *Moros i Cristians*, mock battle, 2 Aug

**Municipal Museum**
📍 Carrer Guillem Cifrede Colonya
☎ 971 531166
🕐 Jul–Sep, Tue–Sat 10–1, 5.30–8.30, Sun 10–1; Oct–Jun, Tue–Sun 11–1
💶 Cheap

*Climbing the Calvari steps on the way to salvation, with Puig de Maria in the background*

39

## Port de Pollença

### INFORMATION

➕ D1

🍴 Choice of restaurants
   (€€)

🚌 From Palma, Pollença and
   Alcúdia; also from Port
   d'Alcúdia and Cap de
   Formentor in summer

🔄 Alcúdia (➤ 24),
   Formentor (➤ 27),
   Pollença (➤ 39)

❓ Market held Wed

**The ambience of Port de Pollença was captured by British crime writer Agatha Christie in *Problem at Pollensa Bay* (1936); its waterfront hotels were favoured by those in search of casual flirtations on the beach.**

This genteel, old-fashioned resort at the mouth of Pollença bay is popular with families, older visitors in winter and is a wheelchair friendly place. There is also a large community of foreign residents, mostly retired British. The promenade along Passeig Voramar, all whitewashed villas and pine trees leaning into the sea, is perfect for an early evening walk. Look for the bust of Hermen Anglada-Camarasa, the Catalan painter who spent many years in Pollença and whose work is displayed in the Fundació la Caixa in Palma (➤ 36). A good walk from Port de Pollença is the 3km hike across the Formentor peninsula through the Bóquer valley, a paradise for ornithologists and lovers of wild flowers.

*The brightly coloured sails of dinghies line the beach at Port de Pollença*

## Puig de Randa

**The steep ascent to Puig de Randa's three hermitages is repaid by the chance to experience the sense of awe and sanctity that still surrounds this table mountain rising 543m out of the plain.**

This mountain has been a place of pilgrimage ever since Ramón Llull (➤ 9) founded Mallorca's first hermitage here in 1275. He came aged 40, shaken by an incident which caused him to review his way of life. Bent on seduction he chased a married woman through Palma; unable to shake him off, she lifted her blouse to reveal cancerous breasts. Llull retired in isolation to Puig de Randa to ponder a life of youthful excess. These days pilgrims here are as likely to be weekend cyclists in search of a challenge as seekers after religious truth. The winding road to the summit leads to three separate hermitages. The lowest, Oratori de Nostra Senyora de Gràcia, is perched on a ledge in the cliff above a sheer 200m drop. Further up is the Santuari de Sant Honorat and finally Santuari de Cura, where Llull lived. The sense of history is offset by the radio mast on the mountain-top and the electric candles in the church, but this is still a special place. Visit the Sala Gramàtica to see Llull's original manuscripts and a bottle of 1934 Chartreuse made in the monastery, then look out from the terrace at the views of the plain, with Palma Bay and the isle of Cabrera in the distance.

**INFORMATION**

➕ D3
☎ 971 120260
🍴 Restaurant at Santuari de Cura (€€)
🎟 Free
❓ Simple rooms are available in a modern pilgrims' block

*Ramón Llull, who retreated to a life of seclusion at the hermitage of Puig de Randa*

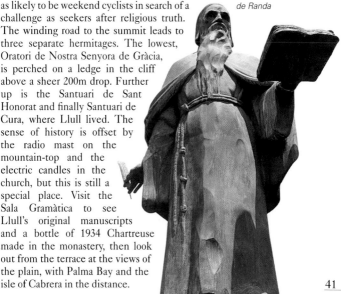

# S'Albufera

## INFORMATION

- D1–D2
- ✉ Carretera Port d'Alcúdia–Artà, km5
- ☎ 971 892250; www.mallorcaweb.net/salbufera
- ◷ Apr–Sep, daily 9–6; Oct–Mar, daily 9–5
- 🍴 Picnic area
- 🚌 From Port d'Alcúdia to Cala Rajada in summer
- 💶 Free
- ↔ Alcúdia (➤ 24)
- ❓ Cars are not allowed in the reserve – leave them 1km from the visitor centre on the main road in the car park opposite Hotel Parc Natural

*Get away from it all with a day at S'Albufera, walking among the marshes and listening to the birds*

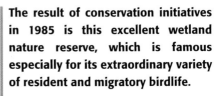

**The result of conservation initiatives in 1985 is this excellent wetland nature reserve, which is famous especially for its extraordinary variety of resident and migratory birdlife.**

Just off the coast road 5km south of Port d'Alcúdia, the S'Albufera wetlands make a welcome relief from long stretches of crowded beach. Birdwatchers come from all over Europe to see rare migrants like Montagu's harriers and Eleanora's falcons; species breeding here include stonechats, moustached warblers and the long-eared owl. Ospreys leave their breeding sites on the cliffs to come here to fish; peregrines and hoopoes live here all year round. The name S'Albufera derives from the Arabic for 'lagoon', but the site has been exploited since Roman times – Pliny writes of night herons, probably from S'Albufera, being sent to Rome as a gastronomic delicacy. The wetlands were drained for agriculture in the 19th century by a British company which subsequently went bankrupt; the network of canals dates from this time. Rice was introduced in the early 20th century, paper was manufactured from the reeds and sedge, and it is only since 1985, following fears that tourist development was damaging the area's fragile ecology, that S'Albufera has been a protected nature reserve. There

are footpaths, cycle trails, birdwatching hides and an audio-visual display room where you can listen to birdsong.

## Sa Calobra

**Once accessible only by sea, the small cove of Sa Calobra can now be reached via a remarkable winding road, making the journey almost as spectacular as the destination.**

Do not believe anyone who tells you that they have discovered the perfect unspoilt cove on the north coast – at least, not if its name is Sa Calobra. This is indeed a beautiful spot, but it cannot be described as secluded – buses filled with tourists pour in by the dozen every day, even in winter.

The journey to Sa Calobra is as memorable as the bay itself. A twisting road around Puig Major plunges 800m in just 12km, turning 270 degrees at one point to loop under itself (a feature known as the 'Knotted Tie'). The easier approach is by boat from Port de Sóller, passing genuinely isolated bays with an excellent view of Puig Major, albeit spoilt by the military installations on the summit of Mallorca's highest mountain.

Once there, walk through 200m of tunnels to reach the Torrent de Pareis ('twin streams'), which begins several kilometres up in the mountains at the confluence of the torrents of Lluc and Gorg Blau. Up to 400m high and only 30m wide, with some sections never seeing daylight, this dramatic gorge culminates in a small pebble beach where you can picnic among the crowds. In summer, when the gorge is dry, you can hike inland between the cliffs; do not attempt this in winter.

A side turn off the road to Sa Calobra leads to Cala Tuent, a small cove with a sandy beach and a 13th-century church, Ermita de Sant Llorenç. Cala Tuent is likely to be quieter than Sa Calobra; but don't believe anyone who tells you they have discovered the real unspoilt cove…

**INFORMATION**

- C1
- Several restaurants (€–€€)
- From Port de Sóller (all year ☎ 971 630170)
- Lluc (► 33), Port de Sóller (► 55)

# Serra de Tramuntana

### INFORMATION

🔲 B2–C2
🔄 Lluc (➤ 33), Fornalutx
(➤ 50), Sa Calobra
(➤ 43), Sóller (➤ 46)
❓ The area is ideal for
walking, birdwatching
and viewing the spring
flowers

**The 'mountains of the north wind', which run the length of Mallorca's north coast, contain some of the island's most spectacular landscapes.**

The pine-covered slopes of the Serra de Tramuntana almost lean into the sea; as you climb higher, forested hills give way to barren crags and peaks. The people of Mallorca have good reason to be grateful to the mountains. In winter they act as a buffer, shielding the plain from the fierce *tramuntana* wind and absorbing most of the island's rain and snow; in summer they provide a cool retreat from the heat of Palma and the south.

*The Gorg Blau reservoir in the Serra de Tramuntana mountains*

The Serra de Tramuntana runs for 88km from Andratx to Pollença, with the rocky outcrops of Sa Dragonera and Cap de Formentor at either end. Of ten peaks over 1,000m, most are concentrated in the area around Lluc; the highest are Puig Major (1,445m) and Puig Massanella (1,349m). There are no rivers, though there are several mountain torrents which swell rapidly after rain – the Cúber and Gorg Blau reservoirs are essential resources on an island so often affected by drought.

The mountains are best explored slowly, on foot; you can smell the wild rosemary, hear the sheep-bells, see the goats, breathe in the air and marvel at pine trees growing out of red rock, nature's version of the colours of Mallorcan village houses. Take care when driving – these are the most dangerous roads on the island, with an endless procession of hairpin bends. The most dramatic drive of all is the C710 from Sóller to Lluc, traversing tunnels and gorges on its way from Puig Major to Puig Massanella.

# Sineu

**A lively weekly market takes over the town of Sineu – observe or join in the enthusiastic haggling, then visit the art gallery in the converted station.**

Sineu, at the geographical centre of Mallorca, comes alive each Wednesday morning at the island's most traditional market. It takes place on several levels. The sound of bleating leads you to the livestock market, where weather-beaten farmers haggle over the price of sheep before heading for the town's *celler* restaurants for an early brunch. Further up, on the way to the church, you pass the symbol of Sineu, a winged lion; near here are numerous stalls selling leather, lace and pearls. Eventually you reach Sa Plaça, the church square, where the action is liveliest of all, as housewives turn out to buy the week's food. Bags of snails, strings of tomatoes, buckets of olives – they are all here, as well as plenty of fresh fruit, colourful vegetables and eye-catching flowers. It's best to get to Sineu early, before the tour buses arrive, to catch the flavour of a traditional country market. Among the best buys at the market are dried figs and apricots, pottery from Pòrtol and baskets – surprisingly, from Sudan. Also in Sineu is **S'Estació**, an unusual modern art gallery based in the old station.

## INFORMATION

➕ D2
🍴 Several restaurants (€€)
🚌 From Palma
❓ Market held Wed

**S'Estació**
✉ Carrer Estació 2
☎ 971 520750;
www.sineuestacio.com
🕐 Mon–Fri 9.30–1.30, 4–7,
Sat 9.30–1
💶 Free

*The winged lion, honouring St Mark, is the symbol of Sineu*

# Sóller

## INFORMATION

✚ C2

🍴 Wide choice of bars and restaurants (€–€€)

🚆 From Palma; tram to Port de Sóller

🔄 Fornalutx (▶ 50), Port de Sóller (▶ 55)

❓ Market held Sat; *Moros i Cristians*, re-enactment of a 1561 battle in which local women helped to defeat a band of Turkish pirates, 8–10 May

**Natural Science Museum**

✉ Carretera Palma–Port de Sóller

☎ 971 634064

🕐 Tue–Sat 10–6, Sun 10–2

💰 Cheap

**Museu de Sóller**

✉ Carrer de Sa Mar 9

☎ 971 634663

🕐 Mon–Fri 11–4, Sat 11–1

💰 Donation

**Set in a lush valley of orange groves between mountains and sea, Sóller is popular with day-trippers, who arrive on the vintage train from Palma.**

Visitors to Sóller from Palma (▶ 34) seem content to do little but sit outside the cafés in Plaça Constitució soaking up the atmosphere and the sun. With several *tapas* bars to choose from, and a fine selection of pastry-shops offering local ice cream and freshly squeezed orange juice, once you arrive here there is little temptation to move on.

The results of Sóller's wealth can be seen in its extravagant *modernista* architecture. The church of Sant Bartomeu has a 1912 arched tower suspended above the rose window, with spires like huge needles pointing into the air. The same architect, Gaudí's pupil Joan Rubió, designed the Banco Central Hispano next door.

A stroll to the cemetery above the station gives a clue to Sóller's history. Several of the epitaphs are in French, revealing the significant French community, descendants of those who came to make their fortune by exporting oranges.

Sóller has two museums worth visiting. The **Natural Science Museum**, in a turn-of-the-19th-century manor house on the Palma road, has a collection of fossils and a botanical garden. The **Museu de Sóller** is an 18th-century house in the town centre, filled with antiques and relics of old Sóller.

A final word of advice: it is advisable to make your visit to Sóller by train, rather than by car. The climb over the Coll de Sóller is the most terrifying drive in Mallorca – it includes 57 hairpin bends. A controversial new road tunnel now runs through the mountain, but the train journey from Palma is a real delight, so why not leave the car behind and give yourself a treat?

## Son Marroig

**The former home of Archduke Ludwig Salvator has now become a lasting memorial to one whose devotion to Mallorca is legendary.**

Of all the famous foreigners attracted to Mallorca's northwest coast, none is so admired locally as 'S'Arxiduc', Archduke Ludwig Salvator. Born in 1847 in the Pitti Palace, Florence, the son of Leopold III of Tuscany and Marie Antoinette de Bourbon, he came to Mallorca 20 years later to escape from Viennese court life and immediately fell in love with the island. An ecologist before it was fashionable, and an early hippy who wore Mallorcan peasant clothes, he bought up estates along the coast in an effort to save them from development, and devoted himself to studying and recording Mallorcan wildlife and traditions. His seven-volume *Las Baleares* took 20 years to produce and is still an authority on its subject. He died in 1915 in a Bohemian castle.

The Archduke's home at Son Marroig, outside Deià, has been turned into a shrine to his memory, with his photographs, paintings and books and a museum devoted to his life. In the gardens is a white marble rotunda, made from Carrara marble and imported from Italy, where you can sit and gaze at the Na Foradada ('pierced rock') peninsula, jutting out to sea with a gaping 18m hole at its centre. Ask at the house for permission to walk onto the peninsula.

### INFORMATION

- ✛ B2
- ✉ Carretera Valldemossa–Deià
- ☎ 971 639158
- 🕐 Apr–Sep, Mon–Sat 10–7.30; Oct–Mar, Mon–Sat 10–5.30
- 🍴 Mirador de Na Foradada (€€)
- 🚌 From Palma, Valldemossa and Port de Sóller
- 💶 Cheap
- ↔ Deià (➤ 30)

*From the rotunda in the Archduke's garden you can look down over the peninsula of Na Foradada*

# Valldemossa

## INFORMATION

➕ B2

🍴 Restaurants and bars (€€)

🚌 From Palma, Deià and Port de Sóller

❓ Regular Chopin concerts in Palau del Rei Sanç (same ticket as monastery); La Beata procession in honour of Santa Catalina Thomás, 27–28 Jul; Chopin Festival in Aug; market held Sun

**Reial Cartoixa**

☎ 971 612106

🕐 Mar–Oct, Mon–Sat 9.30–6, Sun 10–1; Nov–Feb, Mon–Sat 9.30–4.30

💶 Expensive

*Locally-produced oranges are strung around a tree in Valldemossa's market*

**Valldemossa is the focus of the 'Chopin experience' in Mallorca, but it has more to offer, including an excellent modern art museum housed within a Carthusian monastery.**

Try as it might – and it doesn't try very hard – Valldemossa cannot escape its connection with Frédéric Chopin and his lover George Sand. They arrived in 1838, having rented a former monk's cell, planning to carry on their affair away from the gossip of Paris and hoping that the climate would benefit Chopin's health (he had tuberculosis). Nothing worked out as they had intended. The weather was wet and windy, the couple were shunned by the locals, Chopin's piano failed to arrive and the relationship never recovered. Sand vented her anger in a spiteful book, *Winter in Majorca*, which the locals, who were labelled as thieves and savages by the author, still gleefully sell to visitors.

In the **Reial Cartoixa** (Royal Carthusian Monastery) white-arched corridors lead to 'cells' containing museums on various themes. Visit the old pharmacy – you can almost smell the herbs – then look into the library, where the monks would meet for half an hour a week, their only human contact. There is a fine modern art museum, with works by Picasso, Miró and Juli Ramis, and of course there is Chopin's cell…

Valldemossa is also the birthplace of Catalina Thomás, Mallorca's patron saint. Born in 1531, she became a nun in Palma and was renowned for her humility. Almost every home in Valldemossa has a plaque imploring her prayers, and her birthplace at Carrer Rectoría 5 has been turned into a shrine. She would probably be appalled.

The newest attraction in Valldemossa is Michael Douglas' Costa Nord (▶ 78).

# MALLORCA's
## best

Small Towns and Villages *50–51*

Hermitages and Sacred Sites *52*

Historic Sites *53*

Resorts *54–55*

Children's Activities *56–57*

Scenic Places *58*

Free Attractions *59*

Places to Have Lunch *60*

49

# Small Towns and Villages

In the Top 25

**1** ALCÚDIA (➤ 24)
**7** DEIÀ (➤ 30)
**16** POLLENÇA (➤ 39)
**22** SINEU (➤ 45)
**23** SÓLLER (➤ 46)
**25** VALLDEMOSSA (➤ 48)

## CAPDEPERA

This small town is crowned by the largest fortress in Mallorca. The Romans built the first castle on this site – the Moors enlarged it, the Christians destroyed it, then replaced it with one of their own in the 14th century. Legend has it that the besieged citizens of Capdepera hid in the castle, placing an image of Our Lady of Hope on the battlements, and the invaders were driven away by fog. The miracle is remembered each year at the town's annual *festa*. You reach the castle by climbing the steps from the market square.

🔢 F2 🍴 Café de l'Orient, Plaça de l'Orient (€) 🚌 From Palma and Cala Rajada ❓ Market held Wed; Nostra Senyora de la Esperança *festa*, 18 Dec

**Castle** ☎ 971 818746 🕐 Apr–Oct, daily 9–8; Nov–Mar, daily 9–5 💰 Cheap

## FORNALUTX

Fornalutx, in the hills above Sóller, calls itself the prettiest village in Spain, and it is hard to disagree. There are several terrace restaurants and bars, where you can sit and soak up the views of olive and orange groves climbing ever higher until they reach the pine-clad foothills of Puig Major.

🔢 C2 🍴 Several restaurants (€€)

*Is Fornalutx the prettiest village in Spain? Go and judge for yourself*

## GALILEA

This pretty village, 460m above sea level, in the shadow of the great peak of Puig de Galatzó, is popular with day-trippers. From the church terrace you can see far out to sea, while eating *tapas* outside the church and listening to the echo of sheep-bells on the hillsides. The nearby village of Puigpunyent, surrounded by orange groves, is the base for visiting the nature reserve of La Reserva.

🔢 B2 🍴 Two bars (€)

## INCA

Mallorca's third-largest town styles itself 'city of leather'. The best bargains can be found on Thursdays, at the weekly market around Plaça d'Espanya. There is plenty of leather here, of varying quality, plus jewellery, carved olive-wood, lace and fresh produce from across the island. Plaça d'Espanya itself becomes an open-air flower show. Inca is also known for its *cellers*, old wine-cellars turned into restaurants featuring some excellent traditional dishes at reasonable prices.

➕ C2 🍴 Wide choice of restaurants (€€) 🚍 From Palma
🚉 From Palma 🔄 Binissalem ❓ Market held Thu

## MURO

Muro's overriding attraction is the Museu Etnòlogic de Mallorca, which gives fascinating glimpses into Mallorca's past. The kitchen contains pottery similar to what you see in the markets today; the recreated pharmacy has a pair of scales in the shape of a crucifix. Upstairs there is a fine collection of *siurells* (clay whistles) featuring men on horseback.

Sa Pobla, 4km north of Muro, is Mallorca's vegetable basket; this fertile area of reclaimed marshes is referred to as 'the land of a thousand windmills'. It is also the home of one of Mallorca's most unusual festivals, the Revelta de Sant Antoni.

➕ D2 🍴 Bars and cafés (€) 🚉 From Palma ❓ Market held Sun; Revelta de Sant Antoni, 16–17 Jan

**Museu Etnòlogic de Mallorca**

✉ Carrer Major 15 ☎ 971 717540 🕐 Tue, Wed, Fri, Sat 10–3, Sun 10–2 💲 Cheap

## ORIENT

One of Mallorca's tiniest hamlets, with a population of less than 30, Orient nestles among olive trees at the foot of Puig d'Alfábia. Numerous walks start from here, including an ascent to Castell d'Alaró; weekend day-trippers come from Palma to visit its three restaurants for Sunday lunch.

➕ C2 🍴 Three good restaurants (€€)
🔄 Castell d'Alaró (▶ 28)

## PETRA

This sleepy town of sand-coloured houses would be completely off the tourist map if it were not for the fact that it is the birthplace of Mallorca's most famous son, Fray Junípero Serra. Born in 1713, he worked as a missionary first in Mexico and then in California, where the missions he established grew into cities such as San Diego and San Francisco. You can visit the house where Serra's parents lived, a museum devoted to his life and work, the nearby San Bernardino convent where he went to school and a dedication plaque outside the parish church.

➕ D2 🍴 Es Celler restaurant (€€); bars on main square (€)
🚉 From Palma 🔄 Ermita de Bonany (▶ 52) ❓ Market held Wed

**Serra House and Museum**

**Casa Museo Fray Junípero Serra**

✉ Carrer Barracar Alt 6–8–10 ☎ 971 561149
🕐 By arrangement – follow the directions to the keyholder's house
💲 Donation requested

*The house in Petra where Junípero Serra was born has been preserved to look much as it would have done in the 18th century*

51

# Hermitages and Sacred Sites

**In the Top 25**

**10** LLUC (➤ 33)
**18** PUIG DE RANDA (➤ 41)

## ERMITA DE BONANY

This hilltop hermitage is where Junípero Serra preached his last sermon in Mallorca before leaving to found the Mexican and Californian missions. The views from the terrace, covering almost the entire plain, are superb. You can stay here in simple cells, but unlike other monasteries it has no restaurant or bar – just a chapel and a shop selling religious trinkets.

🔳 D2 ☎ 971 561101 💷 Free 🚌 Petra (➤ 51)

## PUIG DE MARIA

Climb for an hour or two out of Pollença, or drive up a terrifying potholed road, and you are rewarded with views over Cap de Formentor and the entire northeastern coast. Nuns settled on Puig de Maria ('Mary's Mountain') in 1371 and remained for several hundred years, refusing to leave even when the Bishop of Palma ordered them down for their own safety. The convent is still there, on top of the mountain; the chapel smells of incense and the refectory of woodsmoke. You can stay in simple rooms in the sanctuary here, but don't expect luxury – you pay extra if you take a shower.

🔳 D1 ☎ 971 184132 🍴 Bar-restaurant (€) 🚌 From Palma to Pollença 💷 Free 🚌 Pollença (➤ 39)

*The views from the Santuari de Sant Salvador stretch right across the central plain*

## SANTUARI DE SANT SALVADOR

This old hermitage, 509m above sea level at the highest point of the Serra de Llevant, was the senior house of Mallorca's monastic order and the last to lose its monks, in 1992. It is still a popular place of pilgrimage, flanked by two enormous landmarks – to one side a 14m stone cross, to the other a 35m column topped by a statue of Christ holding out his right hand in blessing. The church contains a fine carved alabaster retable, but more interesting is the side chapel off the gatehouse, full of poignant mementos and prayers to Our Lady. Like other former monasteries, San Salvador has a few simple rooms available for pilgrims.

🔳 E3 ✉ Signposted from Felanitx–Porto Colom road ☎ 971 827282 🍴 Bar-restaurant (€) and picnic tables 💷 Free

# Historic Sites

> **In the Top 25**
>
> **8** FUNDACIÓ PILAR I JOAN MIRÓ (➤ 31)
> **9** LA GRANJA (➤ 32)
> **12** PALMA'S CASTELL DE BELLVER (➤ 35)
> **14** PALMA'S LA SEU (➤ 37)
> **15** PALMA'S PALAU DE L'ALMUDAINA (➤ 38)

## CAPOCORB VELL

These are the most significant remains of the Talaiotic culture, which flourished in Mallorca between around 1300 and 800 BC. Villages were dominated by *talaiots*, circular or rectangular structures two to three storeys high, which were used as both burial chambers and defensive forts. At Capocorb Vell you can see five *talaiots* and wander around the ancient village.

🔲 C3 ☒ Carretera Cap Blanc–Llucmajor ☎ 971 180155 🕐 Fri–Wed 10–5 🍴 Nearby (€) ♿ Cheap

## PALMA'S BANYS ÀRABS (ARAB BATHS)

These 10th-century baths are virtually all that remain of the Arab city of Medina Mayurqa; they were probably part of a nobleman's house. The *tepidarium* has a dome in the shape of a half-orange, with 25 round shafts for sunlight, supported by a dozen columns. *Hammams* were meeting places as well as wash-houses, and it would have been pleasant to cool off in the courtyard with its cactus, palm and orange trees.

🔲 B2 ☒ Carrer Can Serra 7 ☎ 971 721549 🕐 Apr–Nov, daily 9–7.30; Dec–Mar 9–6 🍴 Bar Sa Murada nearby (€) ♿ None ♿ Cheap

## PALMA'S BASÍLICA DE SANT FRANCESC

The façade of this 13th-century church is typically Mallorcan – a massive, forbidding sandstone wall with a delicately carved portal and a rose window at the centre. Inside is the tomb of Ramón Llull (➤ 41), whose statue can be seen on the seafront at Palma.

🔲 B2 ☒ Plaça Sant Francesc ☎ 971 712695 🕐 Mon–Sat 9.30–12.30, 3.30–6, Sun 9.30–12.30 ♿ Cheap

## SES PAÏSSES

Although not as extensive as the ruins at Capocorb Vell (➤ above), this Bronze Age settlement near Artà is still a significant site, with its massive entrance portal, formed from three stone slabs weighing up to eight tonnes each. Inside there are several rooms and an *atalaia* (watchtower); the entire settlement is surrounded by a Cyclopean drystone wall.

🔲 E2 ☎ 619 070010 🕐 Apr–Oct, Mon–Sat 9.30–1, 4–7.30; Nov–Mar, Mon–Fri 9–1, 2–5 🚌 From Cala Rajada or Palma then a short walk 🔄 Artà (➤ 25) ♿ Cheap

**ART HISTORY**

Mallorca's most important museum, Museu de Mallorca, is housed in a 17th-century palace, with collections spanning more than 3,000 years of history. Start in the basement with the prehistory section, which includes artefacts from the Talaiotic cultures, as well as bronze figures of naked warriors brought back from the Punic wars. Other rooms are devoted to Islamic archaeology, Modernism and 20th-century art.
☒ Carrer Portella 5 ☎ 971 717540 🕐 Tue–Sat 10–7, Sun 10–2 🍴 Bar Sa Murada (€) at foot of Carrer Portella ♿ Cheap

*An impressive baroque portal gives relief to the stern façade of Palma's mighty Basílica de Sant Francesc*

# Mallorca's Best

## Resorts

─── **In the Top 25** ───
4 **CAP DE FORMENTOR** (► 27)
17 **PORT DE POLLENÇA** (► 40)
20 **SA CALOBRA** (► 43)

### PORT D'ALCÚDIA

The biggest of the resorts on Mallorca's northeast coast, it stands at the head of a 10-km stretch of sandy beach that continues around the bay of Alcudia as far as Can Picafort. The area around the fishing harbour is the most attractive; the promenade on Passeig Maritim faces a row of fish restaurants. Near here is the commercial port, where passenger ferries leave for the Menorcan city of Ciutadella.

🔢 D1 🍴 Wide choice of restaurants (€€) 🚌 From Palma and Alcúdia; also from Port de Pollença in summer

### FACILITIES FOR VISITORS WITH DISABILITIES

Sea bathing chairs are available free of charge at several beaches in the Calvia municipality, including the resorrts of Peguera, Santa Ponsa, Magaluf, Palma Nova and Illettes. Further details can be obtained from the Social Welfare Office.

✉ 971 139139

### CALA D'OR

Each of the various *calas* (bays) along the east coast has its own distinctive character; in the case of Cala d'Or the word is 'chic'. Former fishing harbours have been turned into marinas; people come here to sail and dive, and drink champagne at waterfront bars. The villas are white and flat-roofed, in Ibizan style, designed in the 1930s by Pep Costa Ferrer, and the effect is surprisingly attractive. Nowadays Cala d'Or is the collective name for a string of resorts, beaches and coves; they include Porto Petro, around a horseshoe bay 2km to the south, and Cala Mondragó, a further 4km south, where a pair of sandy beaches form part of the Mondragó nature reserve.

🔢 E3 🍴 Wide choice of restaurants (€€–€€€) 🚌 From Palma

### CALA FIGUERA

More than anywhere else in Mallorca, Cala Figuera retains the atmosphere of a working fishing port. A path follows around the tiny harbour and onto the cliffs, offering good views back towards the bay. The nearest beach is 4km to the south at Cala Santanyí.

🔢 E3 🍴 Several seafood restaurants and others (€€) 🚌 From Palma and Santanyí

### PALMA NOVA

There are people who can remember when this was just a village; then along came the tourist boom, and 'new Palma' became the favoured resort of the British. More restrained than Magaluf, less exclusive than Portals Nous, Palma Nova occupies a prime position on the western side of the bay of Palma. It makes a good base for a family holiday, with nearby attractions including Marineland and Aqualand Magaluf (► 56–57) – as long as you don't mind sharing your family holiday with a thousand others.

🔢 B3 🍴 Wide choice of restaurants (€–€€) 🚌 Regular buses from Palma ↔ Magaluf, Portals Nous (► 26)

### PORT D'ANDRATX

Dress up to come here, or you will feel seriously out of place. Port d'Andratx is one of Mallorca's classiest

Port d'Andratx, favourite haunt of the yachting set

resorts, popular with the yachting fraternity and with film stars whose Italian-style villas can be seen climbing up the hillsides. But don't let that put you off; come here all the same. The harbour is one of the prettiest in Mallorca and a table at one of the waterside bars is really the perfect place to watch the sunset.

🚌 A3 🍴 Wide choice of restaurants (€€–€€€) 🚍 From Andratx

### PORT DE SÓLLER

This small resort, set around a fish-shaped natural harbour, has the only beach of any note along the northwestern coast. It is the starting point for several boat trips along the coast; the trip to Sa Calobra (► 43) is one of the few to run throughout the year. Port de Sóller is also a good base for walks. A climb of less than an hour brings you to Cap Gros lighthouse for panoramic views of the bay and the mountains behind; a longer path, through rock gardens and olive groves, connects with an old mule track from Deià to Sóller.

🚌 B2 🍴 Wide choice of restaurants (€€) 🚍 From Palma, Valldemossa and Deià 🚋 From Palma; tram from Sóller

### PORTO CRISTO

This was one of the main resorts on the east coast until Cala Millor came along. So much the better: with bigger and better beaches elsewhere, Porto Cristo has carved out a role as a friendly, family resort, taking advantage of a superb position at the end of a long, sheltered inlet. Once the port for Manacor, Porto Cristo was the only place in Mallorca to be caught up in the Spanish Civil War, when it was briefly captured by Republican forces in 1936. There is not much to do but swim, sunbathe and dine at the terrace restaurants that are perfectly placed to catch the lunchtime sun – but day-trippers come in droves to visit the nearby caves (► 58). Other nearby family attractions include an aquarium and a safari park (► 56–57).

🚌 E2–E3 🍴 Wide choice of restaurants (€€) 🚍 From Palma and Manacor 🚇 Coves del Drac (► 58)
❓ Market held Sun

### SANT ELM

The main reason for visiting Sant Elm, a laid-back resort with a fine sandy beach, is for the views of the island of Sa Dragonera, said to resemble a dragon. You can take a boat to the island from the jetty at the end of the main street, or sit outside the fish restaurants on the same jetty.

🚌 A2 🍴 Choice of restaurants (€€)
🚍 From Andratx or Peguera 🚢 From Port d'Andratx and Peguera in summer 🚇 Sa Dragonera (► 55)

### CALA DE SANT VICENÇ

This old-fashioned holiday resort has recently been given a facelift and is in danger of becoming chic. It is still very popular with Mallorcans, especially on summer weekends. Four small coves, each with their own beach, huddle together beneath Cavall Bernat, a limestone ridge which casts its shadow into the sea. A walk of around 45 minutes leads across the hills to Port de Pollença (► 40).

🚌 D1 🍴 Bars and restaurants (€–€€€) 🚍 Bus from Pollença

*From Sant Elm you can climb to an abandoned monastery or take a boat to Sa Dragonera*

# Children's Activities

Mallorca is well geared up for family holidays. There are lots of good sandy beaches with safe, shallow water and first-aid stations, and many of the resorts feature activities like crazy-golf courses and pony rides. Here is a selection of activities that will appeal to children.

## FAMILY OUTINGS

As well as the attractions listed here, children will enjoy visits to La Granja (➤ 32) and to the various caves along the east coast with their phantasmagorical light displays (➤ 29, 58). The Sóller train and tram ride (➤ 16) makes a fun day out, and the beach at Platja de Palma is very child-friendly with its seafront 'train', shallow water and Red Cross beach stations.

## A WARNING

Note that the attractions listed on this page are among the most expensive in Mallorca.

*Splash-down at Aqualand, one of Mallorca's best children's attractions*

## THEME PARKS AND WATERPARKS

### AQUALAND EL ARENAL
One of the world's largest water funfairs near El Arenal beach. Attractions include an exciting ride where bathers slide down two water slides on a small plastic dinghy and aquaplane into the pool – and Polynesia, a thematic pool with water jets and slides.
➕ C3 ✉ S'Arenal (Platja de Palma); at end of Palma–S'Arenal motorway ☎ 971 440000 ⏰ Daily 10–5 🚌 23 from Palma via Platja de Palma

### AQUALAND MAGALUF
There are pools, slides, a 'water castle' and exciting rides at this long-established waterpark situated on the edge of town. Popular attractions include the Tornado, a tubular water slide that sweeps you down a giant funnel and whirls you down to the pool and the Enchanted Castle guarded by a 15m dragon.
➕ B3 ✉ Carretera Cala Figuera, Magaluf ☎ 971 130811 ⏰ May–Oct, daily 10–6

### HIDROPARK
A water-based theme park with activities for very young children as well as waterslides and wave pools.
➕ D1 ✉ Avinguda Tucán, Port d'Alcúdia ☎ 971 891672 ⏰ May–Oct, daily 10.30–6

### WESTERN PARK
'Crazy Wet West' is the slogan of this Wild West theme park in Magaluf, with cowboy and high-diving shows, thrilling water rides, playgrounds, fast food restaurants and video arcades.
➕ B3 ✉ Carretera Cala Figuera ☎ 971 131203 ⏰ May–Oct, daily 10–6

## ANIMALS AND ZOOS

### ACUÀRIUM DE MALLORCA
A small aquarium with exotic fish from around the world including piranhas and electric eels. Located next to the Coves del Drac (➤ 58).
➕ E3 ✉ Carrer Vella, Porto Cristo ☎ 971 820971 ⏰ Apr–Oct, daily 10.30–6; Nov–Mar, daily 11–3

### GREEN PARK

Reptilarium featuring snakes, crocodiles, tortoises
and iguanas in a modern shopping and entertainment
complex. Reptiles are represented from every
continent including alligators from Africa and
pythons from Central Asia.

✛ C2 ✉ Festival Park, off the Palma-Inca motorway, Marratxí
☎ 971 605481 ⏱ Mon–Fri 10–8, Sat–Sun 10–10

### MARINELAND

Entertainment here is provided by the performing
dolphins, sea lions and parrots. There is also a
penguin pool, a reptile house and a large collection of
sharks and tropical fish, plus flamingos, monkeys and
an impressive aviary. Children can ride on a mock
pirate boat and a miniature train. The little ones will
love it, but their parents may not – especially if they
are fond of dolphins. But whatever you think about
animal shows, Marineland is a success – and the
crowds it attracts generate handsome profits, which
are then put back into conservation programmes.

✛ B3 ✉ Carretera Palma–Andratx km10, Portals Nous ☎ 971
675125 ⏱ Apr–Sep, daily 9.30–6; Oct–Mar, daily 9.30–5. Closed mid-
Nov to Christmas 🚌 From Palma, Palma Nova, Magaluf, Santa Ponça

### NATURA PARC

An easy walking trail leads around a wildlife park
where Mallorcan farm animals can be seen, along
with butterflies, black vultures and imported species
like pelicans and Chinese geese. There is also a
picnic area and café.

✉ Carretera de Sineu, km15 ☎ 971 144078 ⏱ Apr–Oct, daily
10–7; Nov–Mar, daily 10–6

### NEMO SUBMARINES

See the flora and fauna beneath the sea on a 2-hour
exploration by mini-submarine. Very expensive.

✛ B3 ✉ Carrer Galéon 2, Magaluf ☎ 971 130244
⏱ Mar–Oct, daily

### AUTO SAFARI

Drive-round safari park with giraffes, zebra and
monkeys plus a 'baby zoo' with young elephants and
reptiles born here. Arrive early to see the feeding.

✛ F2 ✉ Carretera Porto Cristo–Son Servera, km5, Cala Millor
☎ 971 810909 ⏱ Apr–Sep, daily 9–7; Oct–Mar, daily 9–5
🚌 Free bus service from Cala Millor in summer

## MINI-GOLF

### GOLF FANTASIA (PALMA NOVA)

One of the best mini-golf courses, set amid waterfalls,
caves and tropical gardens. There is a choice of three
different circuits – or you can play all 54 holes. Even
adults will enjoy it.

✛ B3 ✉ Carrer Tenis 3, Palma Nova ☎ 971 682349 ⏱ Daily,
10–midnight

---

**LOOKING AFTER CHILDREN**

Small children are particularly
vulnerable to the sun and
need to be well protected:
apply a high-factor sun block
regularly, especially after
swimming. If you need a child
seat in your rented car, be
sure to book it in advance and
then check it carefully on
arrival. The same goes for cots
and high-chairs in hotels and
apartments. Finally, don't
forget to check that your
balcony railings are secure.

*A trio of performing
dolphins at Marineland*

# Scenic Places

*The terraced slopes of Banyalbufar, created over a thousand years, reach right down to the sea*

**In the Top 25**


4 CAP DE FORMENTOR (➤ 27)
6 COVES D'ARTÀ (➤ 29)
7 DEIÀ (➤ 30)
20 SA CALOBRA (➤ 43)
21 SERRA DE TRAMUNTANA (➤ 44)


### BANYALBUFAR

People come to Banyalbufar to see one thing – its terraced hillsides, sloping down to the sea. Developed by the Moors and divided by drystone walls, these terraces speak powerfully of man's ingenuity in creating farmland out of inhospitable cliffs. Until recently it was the custom for each generation to add a further tier.

B2 Café Bellavista (€) Bus from Palma
La Granja (➤ 32)

### COVES DEL DRAC (DRAGON CAVES)

Dank, dark and humid, these limestone caves on the edge of Porto Cristo have become one of Mallorca's top tourist sights. Several hundred people at a time are herded along 2km of slippery paths by guides; the tour ends with a floodlit, floating violin concert on Lake Martel, which is Europe's largest underground lake.

E3 971 820753 Apr–Oct, tours on the hour 10–5; Nov–Mar, tours at 10.45, 12, 2 Café (€) From Palma and Cala Rajada None Expensive Acuàrium de Mallorca (➤ 56)

### JARDINS DE ALFÁBIA

These classical gardens by the entrance to the Sóller tunnel are a legacy of the Arab talent for landscaping and irrigation. The name derives from *al fabi*, 'jar of olives' in Arabic. They were probably designed by Benihabet, the Muslim governor of Inca who converted to Christianity following the Spanish invasion.

B2 Carretera Palma–Sóller, km17 971 613123
Apr–Sep, Mon–Sat 9.30–6.30; Oct–Mar, Mon–Fri 9.30–5.30, Sat 9.30–1 Ses Porxeres (€€) in the car park Moderate

### PALMA'S PARC DE LA MAR

Until the 1960s the sea reached up to the city walls, providing the perfect reflection for the cathedral. When the building of a new road changed all that, an artificial lake was constructed to reproduce the effect. The park around the lake is now a popular venue at weekends, with a Miró mural and an art gallery in the vaults of the old city walls.

B2 On south side of the cathedral Choice of cafés (€)
Free Free concerts on summer evenings

# Free Attractions

In the Top 25

**2** ARTÀ (➤ 25)
**22** SINEU (➤ 45)

*The furnaces and machinery in the Ca'n Gordiola glass factory are on view to visitors*

### CA'N GORDIOLA
Glass factory and museum, housed in a mock castle outside the town of Algaida. Watch the glass being made, then buy it in the shop next door.
➕ C2 ✉ Carretera Palma-Manacor, km19 ☎ 971 665046
🕐 Jun–Sep, daily 9–8; Oct–May Mon–Sat 9–7, Sun 9–1.30

### CA'N SOLLERIC
This 18th-century seigneurial palace was built for a family of olive oil merchants. It now houses a contemporary art gallery whose ground-floor café is one of the trendiest meeting places in Palma.
➕ B2 ✉ Passeig des Born 27, Palma ☎ 971 722092
🕐 Tue–Sat 10–2, 5–9, Sun 10–1.30

### MUSEU JUNÍPERO SERRA
This small museum devoted to the 'founder of California' (➤ 9) is located in a house close to his birthplace in the village of Petra (➤ 51).
➕ D2 ✉ Carrer Barracar Alt 6–8–10, Petra ☎ 971 561149
🕐 By arrangement – follow directions to the keyholder's house (donation requested)

### PERLAS MAJÓRICA
Cultured pearls are one of Mallorca's best-known exports. Watch them being made at this pearl factory.
➕ E2 ✉ Avinguda Majórica 48, Manacor ☎ 971 550200
🕐 Mon–Fri 9–7, Sat–Sun 10–1

### SES VOLTES
The art gallery in the military vaults of Palma's medieval walls has a comprehensive collection of 19th- and 20th-century Mallorcan paintings.
➕ B2 ✉ Parc de la Mar, Palma ☎ 971 728739
🕐 Jun–Sep, Mon–Sat 10–1.45, 5–8.45, Sun 10–1.45; Oct–May, Mon–Sat 10–5.45

### DOING THE *PASSEIG*

The best free entertainment in Mallorca consists of joining the locals on their early evening promenade (*paseo* in Spanish, *passeig* in Mallorquín). The most romantic *passeig* of all is along the Pine Walk in Port de Pollença, where the pine trees lean into the sea, the fishing boats bob in the bay and the various terrace bars tempt you in for an apéritif beside the beach.

# Places to Have Lunch

**WINE**

Mallorcan wines have been growing in reputation in recent years and several *bodegas* sell direct to the public. If you are lucky you will be able to taste before you buy. Among the best producers are José L Ferrer at Binissalem (☎ 971 511050), Miquel Oliver at Petra (☎ 971 561117) and Jaume Mesquida at Porreres (☎ 971 647106).

### BON LLOC (€)

You won't find better value than this four-course vegetarian lunch.

➕ B2 ✉ Carrer Sant Feliu 7, Palma ☎ 971 718617 🕒 Closed Sun

### CA N'ANTUNA (€€)

Dine on a terrace overlooking the orange groves.

➕ C2 ✉ Carrer Arbona Colom 7, Fornalutx ☎ 971 633068 🕒 Closed Mon

### CELLER SA FONT (€€)

Farmers go here after Sineu's Wednesday market.

➕ D2 ✉ Plaça d'Espanya 18, Sineu ☎ 971 520313 🕒 Daily

### CENTRO (€)

Huge portions, excellent food, ridiculous prices.

➕ D3 ✉ Avinguda Bisbe Campins 13, Porreres ☎ 971 168372 🕒 Closed Sun

### LA GRAN TORTUGA (€€)

Eat and swim on a terrace overlooking the sea.

➕ A3 ✉ Aldea Cala Fornells 1, Peguera ☎ 971 686023 🕒 Closed Mon

### PUIG DE SANT MIQUEL (€€)

Roast kid and other Mallorcan specialities served beside a hilltop sanctuary.

✉ Carretera de Manacor, km31 ☎ 971 646314 🕒 Closed Mon

### TABERNA DE LA BOVEDA (€€)

Great *tapas* on the waterfront in Palma.

➕ B2 ✉ Passeig Sagrera 3, Palma ☎ 971 720026 🕒 Closed Sun

### STAY (€€€)

Fresh fish beside the harbour.

➕ D1 ✉ Moll Nou, Port de Pollença ☎ 971 864013 🕒 Daily

*Holidaymakers and locals enjoy a coffee in Palma's Plaça Major*

# MALLORCA
## where to...

**EAT AND DRINK**
In Palma *62–63*
Around the Island *64–69*

**STAY**
In Palma *70*
Around the Island *71–73*

**SHOP**
Markets *74*
Shopping in Palma *75*
Arts and Crafts in Palma *76*
Arts and Crafts Around
  the Island *77*

**BE ENTERTAINED**
Theatres and Concerts *78*
Bars *79*
Discos and Dinner Shows *80*
Golf Courses *81*
Watersports *82*
Spectator Sports *83*

# In Palma

## PRICES

Prices are approximate, based on a three-course meal for one, without drinks and service:
€ = under €15
€€ = €15–€30
€€€ = over €30
Most restaurants serve a *menú del día* at lunchtime (► 66), which will usually work out much cheaper. It is normal practice to add about 10 per cent to the bill as a tip.

## A WARNING

Opening hours change frequently, and many restaurants take an annual holiday in winter. It is always a good idea to telephone before setting out.

### ARAMIS (€€€)

Modern Mediterranean cuisine and a good-value set lunch in a town house behind La Llotja.
✉ Carrer Montenegro 1
☎ 971 725232 🕐 Lunch, Mon–Fri, dinner Mon–Sat

### BAHÍA MEDITERRÁNEO (€€€)

Top class restaurant reached by lift, known for its top international cuisine. Well-positioned with terrace offering views of the bay of Palma.
✉ Passeig Marítim 33, 5th floor ☎ 971 457653/458877
🕐 Lunch, dinner

### LA BODEGUILLA (€€)

Modern variations of classic Spanish cuisine; the same owners have a stylish *tapas* bar next door.
✉ Carrer Sant Jaume 1 & 3
☎ 971 718274
🕐 Mon–Sat 1–11.30

### BON LLOC (€)

Vegetarian restaurant with four-course set lunch.
✉ Carrer Sant Feliu 7
☎ 971 718617 🕐 Lunch Mon–Sat

### CABALLITO DE MAR (€€)

Popular fish restaurant on the seafront – sit outside to catch the sun.
✉ Passeig Sagrera 5
☎ 971 721074
🕐 Lunch, dinner. Closed Mon

### CA'N CARLOS (€€)

One of the few restaurants in central Palma to focus on traditional Mallorcan cuisine.
✉ Carrer de l'Aigua 5
☎ 971 713869
🕐 Lunch, dinner. Closed Sun

### CANDELA (€€€)

In a street known for its *tapas* bars, this place offers fresh fish and creative Mediterranean cuisine.
✉ Carrer dels Apuntadors 14
☎ 971 724428 🕐 Dinner only. Closed Wed

### CA'N EDUARDO (€€)

Traditional fish restaurant above the fish market.
✉ Travessia Pesquera 4 (Mollet) ☎ 971 721182
🕐 Lunch, dinner. Closed Sun

### CA'N JOAN DE S'AIGO (€)

Classy café where Joan Miró used to go for hot chocolate and *ensaimadas*.
✉ Carrer Sant Sanç 10
☎ 971 710759
🕐 Closed Tue

### CELLER SA PREMSA (€€)

Mallorcan classics in a converted garage lined with wine vats and faded bullfighting posters.
✉ Plaça Bisbe Berenguer de Palou 8 ☎ 971 723529
🕐 Lunch, dinner. Closed Sun

### CHOPIN (€€€)

Top-notch Swiss-Mediterranean dishes on a garden terrace.
✉ Carrer Ca'n Puigdorfila 2
☎ 971 723556
🕐 Lunch Mon–Fri, dinner Mon–Sat

### ES BALAURD (€€€)

Attractive décor, great local favourite. Specialises in innovative Mallorcan dishes, noted for the quality and freshness of the ingredients.
✉ Porta de Santa Catalina
☎ 971 908199
🕐 Lunch, dinner Mon–Sat

**FABRICA 23 (€€)**
One of the hottest restaurants in town run by an English chef in the buzzing Santa Catalina district. Arrive early if you want a table at lunchtime.
✉ Carrer Fabrica 23
☎ 971 728077 ⏰ Lunch, dinner. Closed Sun

**FLOR DE LOTO (€€)**
Intimate bistro offering vegetarian and fish dishes in the back streets around La Llotja.
✉ Carrer Vallseca 7 ☎ 971 717778 ⏰ Dinner Tue–Sun

**FUNDACIÓ LA CAIXA (€€)**
Cocktails, cakes and serious meals in the bar of the former Gran Hotel.
✉ Plaça Weyler 3
☎ 971 728077 ⏰ Lunch, dinner. Closed Sun dinner

**KOLDO ROYO (€€€)**
Specialising in Basque and Mallorcan *nouvelle cuisine*, with views of the bay.
✉ Passeig Marítim 3
☎ 971 732435 ⏰ Lunch Tue–Fri, dinner Tue–Sun

**LA LUBINA (€€)**
Fish restaurant on the quay – try *lubina en sal*, sea bass baked in rock salt.
✉ Es Moll Vell ☎ 971 723350 ⏰ Lunch, dinner

**NA BAUÇANA (€)**
Friendly vegetarian restaurant with set-price midweek lunch.
✉ Carrer Santa Bàrbara 4
☎ 971 721886
⏰ Lunch Mon–Fri

**OPIO (€€)**
Funky 'Mediterrasian' fusion food at an ethnic-style boutique hotel.
✉ Carrer Montenegro 12
☎ 971 425450
⏰ Lunch, dinner Tue–Sun

**EL PILON (€€)**
Good *tapas* bar in an alley off the Born.
✉ Carrer Ca'n Cifre 3
☎ 971 717590
⏰ Lunch, dinner. Closed Sun

**SA LLIMONA (€)**
Create your own *pa amb oli* with a huge choice of toppings. Good salads too.
✉ Carrer Fábrica 27A
☎ 971 736096 ⏰ Lunch, dinner

**SA VOLTA (€)**
Authentic cellar bar with hams hanging from the ceiling – one of numerous *tapas* bars along this street.
✉ Carrer dels Apuntadors 5
⏰ Lunch, dinner Mon–Sat

**TABERNA DE LA BOVEDA (€€)**
Great *tapas* on a terrace facing the harbour.
✉ Passeig Sagrera 3 ☎ 971 720026 ⏰ Lunch, dinner Mon–Sat

**TABERNA DEL CARACOL (€€)**
Great little *tapas* restaurant housed in an old stone building close to the Arab Baths.
✉ Carrer Sant Alonso 2
☎ 971 714908 ⏰ Lunch, dinner. Closed Sun

**TXAKOLI (€€)**
Charcoal-grilled meat is the speciality at this busy Basque joint in the heart of Santa Catalina.
✉ Carrer Fábrica 14 ☎ 971 282126 ⏰ Lunch Mon–Fri, dinner Mon–Sat

*TAPAS*

*Tapas* are a Spanish institution. Originally a free 'lid' (*tapa*) of ham across a drink, nowadays they consist of small portions of everything from octopus to olives. Locals eat *tapas* before going out to eat, but several portions can make an excellent meal in itself. The best place to eat *tapas* in Mallorca is in the area around La Llotja in Palma.

# Around the Island

**EATING OUT IN MALLORCA**

The Spanish like to eat late –
many restaurants do not even
open until 1.30 at lunchtime
and 8.30 in the evening, and
fill up an hour or two later. It is
a good idea to book a table in
advance, especially in summer
and at weekends. Formal
dress is rarely necessary –
even at the best
establishments smart casual is
the rule. And children are
always welcome!

## ALCÚDIA

### SA PLAÇA (€€)

Traditional and modern
Spanish and
Mediterranean cuisine –
how about courgettes
stuffed with pine nuts,
raisins, black pudding and
Mallorcan cheese?
✉ Plaça Constitució 1 ☎ 971
546278 🕐 Thu–Tue 12–12

## ALGAIDA

### CAL DIMONI (€€)

Meat and blood sausages
grilled over an open fire.
✉ Carretera Palma–Manacor,
km21 ☎ 971 665035
🕐 Lunch, dinner. Closed Wed

### CA'N MATEU (€€)

Roast suckling pig and
other specialities; pool and
children's play area.
✉ Carretera Palma–Manacor,
km21 ☎ 971 665036
🕐 Lunch, dinner. Closed Tue

### ES 4 VENTS (€€)

Mallorcan and Spanish
classics, very popular for
Sunday lunch.
✉ Carretera Palma–Manacor,
km21 ☎ 971 665173
🕐 Lunch, dinner. Closed Thu
and part of Jun/Jul

### HOSTAL D'ALGAIDA
(€€)

Mallorcan cuisine in an
old coaching inn – try
croquettes of spinach with
monkfish.
✉ Carretera Palma–Manacor,
km21 ☎ 971 665109
🕐 Lunch, dinner

## ARTÀ

### CAFÉ PARISIEN (€€)

Coffee, pastries, salads
and Mediterrranean
cuisine in an arty café on
the city's main street.
✉ Carrer Ciutat 18 ☎ 971
835440 🕐 Lunch, dinner daily
Closed Wed

## BINISSALEM

### SCOTT'S BISTRO (€€)

Cosy, candlelit ambience
and a menu of freshly
prepared market cuisine –
steaks, fish, vegetables. A
romantic venue.
✉ Carrer Pou Bo 20
☎ 971 870076 🕐 Mon–Sat
7pm–midnight

## CALA RAJADA

### SES ROTGES (€€€)

Quality French cooking
with prices to match, in
the restaurant at one of
Mallorca's top hotels.
✉ Carrer Rafael Blanes 21
☎ 971 563108 🕐 Lunch,
dinner. Closed Nov–Mar

## CALA DE SANT
VIÇENC

### CAVALL BERNAT (€€€)

Top-notch Mallorcan
meat and fish dishes, such
as spiced turbot and roast
suckling lamb, plus
a gourmet tasting menu.
✉ Carrer Maressers 2
☎ 971 530250
🕐 Dinner daily

## CALVIÀ

### MESON CA'N TORRAT
(€€)

Mallorcan classics like
*llom amb col* and roast
shoulder of lamb in a
rustic bar opposite
the church.
✉ Carrer Major 29 ☎ 971
670682 🕐 Lunch, dinner.
Closed Tue

## CAPDEPERA

### CAFÉ DE L'ORIENT (€)

Lively *tapas* bar on the market square – each dish is available in three different-sized portions.

✉ Plaça de l'Orient 4
☎ 971 563098 ⏰ Daily 8am–midnight

## CASTELL D'ALARÓ

### ES VERGER (€€)

Delicious roast lamb cooked in a wood-fired oven at this farmhouse restaurant halfway up to the castle.

✉ On the way to Castell d'Alaró ☎ 971 182126
⏰ Lunch, dinner

## COLÒNIA DE SANT JORDI

### MARISOL (€€)

A good old-fashioned beach terrace right on the harbour, offering fresh fish, paella, pizza and pasta dishes for all the family.

✉ On the harbourside
☎ 971 655070 ⏰ Mar–Oct, lunch and dinner daily

## DEIÀ

### EL OLIVO (€€€)

Fine *nouvelle cuisine* in a romantic setting – one of the best restaurants on the island for a special occasion. There is even a vegetarian gourmet menu.

✉ La Residencia hotel
☎ 971 639392
⏰ Lunch, dinner

### JAUME (€€)

A Deià institution offering unchanging Mallorcan dishes like *tumbet* and *frit mallorquí* in defiance of the trends towards new Mallorcan cuisine.

✉ Carrer Arxiduc Lluis Salvador 24 ☎ 971 639029
⏰ Lunch, dinner. Closed Mon

### MIRADOR DE NA FORADADA (€€)

Dine with a view of the northwest coast. Typical Mallorcan/Spanish cuisine.

✉ Son Marroig, Carretera Valldemossa–Deià
☎ 971 639026
⏰ Lunch, dinner. Closed Thu

## FORNALUTX

### CA'N ANTUNA (€€)

Mallorcan cuisine on a shady terrace with views of orange groves and distant peaks that makes for a great relaxing meal

✉ Carrer Arbona Colom 7
☎ 971 633068 ⏰ Lunch, dinner. Closed Mon

## GÈNOVA

### MESON CA'N PEDRO (€€)

The busiest restaurant in Mallorca turns out huge portions of barbecued meat at generous prices in a village on the outskirts of Palma.

✉ Carrer Rector Vives 14
☎ 971 702162 ⏰ Lunch, dinner. Closed Wed

## INCA

### CELLER CA'N AMER (€€)

This busy *celler* represented the best Balearic cooking at the Expo 92 fair in Seville.

✉ Carrer Pau 39 ☎ 971 501261 ⏰ Lunch, dinner. Closed Sun

### CELLERS

A *celler* is an old wine cellar converted into a restaurant specialising in traditional Mallorcan cuisine. Real basement *cellers* have wine vats to prove it, but nowadays the term is used for any old-style restaurant.

*Cellers* are good places to go in order to try Mallorcan classics like *llom amb col* (pork wrapped in cabbage) or *frit mallorquí* (fried offal). The best *cellers* are found in market towns like Inca and Sineu.

# Around the Island

## MENÚ DEL DÍA

Most restaurants offer a *menú del día* at lunchtime – a set-price three-course meal with water or wine included. You won't get much choice (typically soup or salad, meat or fish and fruit or ice cream) but the food will be freshly cooked, filling and sometimes surprisingly good. A three-course lunch in a small rural town will often cost less than a single portion of *tapas* in Palma.

## JARDINES D'ALFÁBIA

### SES PORXERES (€€)
Catalan game dishes in a rustic barn beside the Alfábia gardens.
✉ Carretera Palma–Sóller
☎ 971 613762 🕐 Lunch, dinner. Closed Sun dinner, Mon

## ORIENT

### DALT MUNTANYA (€€)
*Pa amb oli* at lunchtime and modern Mallorcan cooking in the evening at this newly renovated hotel.
✉ Carretera de Bunyola
☎ 971 615373
🕐 Feb–Oct, lunch, dinner

### L'HERMITAGE (€€€)
Choose between a flower-filled terrace or a dining-room full of antiques at this 17th-century manor house and hotel. The menu, based on fresh local ingredients, changes daily.
✉ Carretera Alaró–Bunyola
☎ 971 180303
🕐 Jan–mid Nov, lunch, dinner

### MANDALA (€€)
Innovative French–Indian cuisine by a couple from Geneva, in a house at the very top of the village.
✉ Carrer Nou 1
☎ 971 615285 🕐 Jun–Aug, dinner Mon–Sat; Sep–May, lunch Tue–Thu, Sun, dinner Fri–Sat

### RESTAURANT ORIENT (€)
Roast lamb, snails and other rustic Mallorcan dishes in this village bar.
✉ Carretera de Bunyola
☎ 971 615153 🕐 Lunch, dinner. Closed Sun dinner, Tue

## PALMA NOVA

### CIRO'S (€€)
Italian and Mediterranean specialities served on a terrace overlooking the beach.
✉ Passeig del Mar 3 ☎ 971 681052 🕐 Lunch, dinner

## PEGUERA

### LA GRAN TORTUGA (€€)
Seafood and European cuisine served on a terrace overlooking a pretty bay. Order your meal and take a dip in the swimming pool while your food is being cooked.
✉ Aldea Cala Fornells 1
☎ 971 686023
🕐 Lunch, dinner. Closed Mon

## PETRA

### ES CELLER (€€)
Typical Mallorcan *celler* bar with an olive press and hearty peasant cooking.
✉ Carrer de l'Hospital 46
☎ 971 561056 🕐 Lunch, dinner. Closed Mon

### SA PLAÇA (€€)
Prawns in chocolate sauce is just one of the old-style Mallorcan dishes being reinvented at this samll hotel-restaurant on the main square.
✉ Plaça Ramon Llull 4
☎ 971 561646 🕐 Lunch, dinner. Closed Tue

## POLLENÇA

### BALAIXA (€€)
Dine on the terrace in summer or indoors in winter at this old Mallorcan farmhouse with

its own private pool on the main road to Port de Pollença.

✉ Carretera Port de Pollença
☎ 971 530659
🕓 Lunch, dinner

### CA'N PACIENCI (€€€)

Sample the adventurous French-style cooking that Ca'n Pacienci has to offer, including duck in five different sauces.

✉ Carretera Port de Pollença
☎ 971 530787
🕓 Mar–Oct, dinner only Mon–Sat

### CANTONET (€€)

Italian restaurant featuring salads, fresh pasta and vegetarian dishes.

✉ Carrer Montesió 20
☎ 971 530429
🕓 Dinner only. Closed Tue

### CLIVIA (€€)

This popular restaurant is in an old manor house – the speciality is roasted sea bass.

✉ Avinguda Pollentia 9
☎ 971 533635
🕓 Lunch, dinner. Closed Wed

### LA FONT DEL GALL (€€)

French-style cooking in an intimate back-street restaurant close to the 'cockerel fountain' from which it takes its unusual name.

✉ Carrer Montesió 4
☎ 971 530396
🕓 Apr–Oct, dinner daily

### IL GIARDINO (€€)

Some good Italian specialities – veal with mushrooms, salmon with lemon sauce.

✉ Plaça Major 11
☎ 971 534302
🕓 Lunch, dinner

### JUMA (€)

A great selection of *tapas* served throughout the day at this old-style hotel on the main square.

✉ Plaça Major 9
☎ 971 533258
🕓 Daily 8am–midnight

## PORT D'ALCÚDIA

### BOGAVANTE (€€€)

The rice and fresh fish dishes are especially good at this seafood restaurant facing the harbour.

✉ Carrer Teodor Canet 2
☎ 971 547364
🕓 Lunch Tue–Sun, dinner daily

### MIRADOR DE LA VICTORIA (€€)

Worth a drive for the sea views from the terrace of this restaurant, by the Santueri de la Victoria. Chicken dishes and grilled rabbit to be recommended.

✉ Cap des Pinar
☎ 971 547171
🕓 Lunch, dinner. Closed Mon and Dec–Jan

## PORT D'ANDRATX

### MIRAMAR (€€€)

Dine on lobster and seafood sitting beside the harbour – but you'll need to take out a mortgage before you come here, the prices are steep.

✉ Avinguda Mateo Bosch 22
☎ 971 671617
🕓 Feb–Sep, lunch, dinner daily

### ROCAMAR (€€)

This is the place to try Galician and Mallorcan seafood specialities in a perfect setting at the end of the promenade.

✉ Carrer d'Almirante Riera Alemany 29
☎ 971 671261
🕓 Lunch, dinner

### FISH AND SEAFOOD

Mallorca's fish stocks have long been in decline and most of the fish on sale in Mallorca is imported from mainland Spain and beyond. By law, restaurant menus should state whether fish is fresh or frozen – prices for frozen fish are invariably cheaper. Fresh fish is always excellent; specialities include lobster casserole, sea bass in rock salt, and *greixonera de peix*, a hearty fish stew cooked in an earthenware bowl.

# Around the Island

## OLIVES

Olives were introduced to Mallorca by the Romans and have been used ever since – the oil for cooking and soap, the branches for firewood, the wood for carving into bowls and spoons. Almost every meal begins with bread and olives, for which you may pay a small charge. Bread and olives are also at the heart of *pa amb oli*, the favourite Mallorcan snack – bread rubbed with tomato, drizzled with olive oil and topped with ham or cheese.

## PORT DE POLLENÇA

### CA'N CUARASSA (€€)
Top-notch Mediterranean cuisine in a delightful setting with views across the bay.
✉ Carretera Port de Pollença-Alcúdia ☎ 971 864266
🕐 Lunch, dinner

### STAY (€€€)
This is a popular fish restaurant on the jetty – try the *parrillada*, a fish and seafood mixed grill.
✉ Moll Nou ☎ 971 864013
🕐 Lunch, dinner

## PORT DE SÓLLER

### CELLER D'ES PORT (€€)
Enormous helpings of Mallorcan classics like roast shoulder of lamb with oregano.
✉ Carrer Antoni Montis 17
☎ 971 630654
🕐 Lunch Thu–Tue, dinner Sat

### ES FARO (€€€)
Fresh fish in a magnificent setting, high above the fishing port.
✉ Cap Gros de Maleta
☎ 971 633752
🕐 Lunch, dinner. Closed Tue in winter

## PORTALS NOUS

### TAHINI (€€€)
There are numerous swanky bistros around the marina at Puerto Portals but this one stands out for its minimalist design and Japanese-inspired fusion food.
✉ Puerto Portals
☎ 971 676025
🕐 Lunch, dinner Tue–Sun

## PORTO COLOM

### CELLER SA SINIA (€€)
Seafood specialities in a perfect spot on the waterfront.
✉ Carrer des Pescadors 25
☎ 971 824323 🕐 Lunch, dinner. Closed Mon

## RANDA

### CELLER BAR RANDA (€)
Good-value Mallorcan cuisine in the village bar beside the church.
✉ Carrer Església 20
☎ 971 660989
🕐 Lunch, dinner. Closed Wed

### ES RECO DE RANDA (€€)
Mallorcan and Spanish cooking in an old hotel at the foot of Puig de Randa.
✉ Carrer Font 13
☎ 971 660997
🕐 Lunch, dinner

## S'ARRACÓ

### LA TULIPE (€€)
Modern European cooking in a New Age arty atmosphere.
✉ Plaça de Toledo 2
☎ 971 671449
🕐 Dinner Mon–Sat

## SANTA MARIA DEL CAMÍ

### CA'N CALET (€€)
Bustling restaurant just off the main road in an old townhouse with stone arches and a pretty garden. You'll find good value Spanish/Mallorcan food.
✉ Plaça dels Hostals 26
☎ 971 620173
🕐 Lunch, dinner

## MOLI D'ES TORRENT (€€€)

Chef Peter Himbert offers a personal interpretation of German and Mallorcan cuisine at this restaurant in an old windmill.

✉ Carretera Bunyola 75
☎ 971 140503  ⏱ Lunch, dinner. Closed Thu, Mon–Sat lunch in Jul and Aug

## READS (€€€)

British chef Marc Fosh conjures up sublime creations such as grilled sea-bass in liquorice sauce at this grand, eccentric country hotel.

✉ Carretera Santa Maria-Alaró
☎ 971 140261
⏱ Lunch, dinner

## SIMPLY FOSH (€€)

If you don't want to splash out, the same chef (► above) offers simpler bistro farc, such as risottos, curries and fish soup, at affordable prices.

✉ Carretera Santa Maria-Alaró
☎ 971 140261
⏱ Lunch, dinner

### SANT ELM

## EL PESCADOR (€€)

Fish restaurant on the jetty with its own fishing boat and fine views of Sa Dragonera.

✉ Avinguda Jaume I
☎ 971 239198
⏱ Lunch, dinner

### SINEU

## CELLER SA FONT (€€)

Traditional *celler* with wine vats lining the walls – very busy on market day.

✉ Plaça d'Espanya 18
☎ 971 520313
⏱ Lunch, dinner

### SÓLLER

## BENS D'AVALL (€€€)

Treat yourself to some creative Mediterranean cuisine in a fabulous setting with views of the northwest coast.

✉ Carretera Deià–Sóller, Urbanización Costa de Deià
☎ 971 632381
⏱ Apr–Nov, lunch Tue–Sun, dinner Tue–Sat

## CA N'AI (€€)

Fine food and elegant service on the terace of a country house hotel surrounded by orange groves.

✉ Carrer Puig Mayor
☎ 971 632494  ⏱ Feb–Oct, lunch, dinner. Closed Mon

## SA COVA (€€)

This restaurant serves Mallorcan classics (stuffed aubergines and rabbit with garlic) in a great position on Sóller's main square.

✉ Plaça Constitució 7
☎ 971 633222
⏱ Lunch, dinner. Closed Sun dinner and Mon

### VALLDEMOSSA

## CA'N COSTA (€€)

Mallorcan and Spanish cuisine served in a converted oil-mill.

✉ Carretera Valldemossa–Deià, km2.5  ☎ 971 612263
⏱ Lunch, dinner. Closed Tue

## VALLDEMOSSA (€€€)

Impeccable service, fine wines and creative Mediterranean cooking in a luxury hotel with a terrace overlooking the village.

✉ Carretera Vieja de Valldemossa  ☎ 971 612626
⏱ Lunch, dinner

## COFFEE AND LIQUEURS

In Spain, *un café* after the meal means only one thing: *café solo*, served short, strong and black, with sugar. Ask for a *carajillo* and it will have brandy added, or a bottle of *coñac* left on the table for you to help yourself. If the waiter brings a liqueur with your coffee, this is a *copa*, a treat on the house. Enjoy!

# In Palma

## PRICES

Prices are for a double room, excluding breakfast and VAT:

€ = under €60
€€ = €60–€120
€€€ = over €120

These prices will be much lower if you book as part of a package holiday. Most hotels in the main resorts are block-booked by tour operators and it is through them that you will get the cheapest deals.

## WHAT DOES IT MEAN?

All accommodation in Spain is strictly classified and graded by the government. Hotels are graded from one to five stars; *hostals*, with fewer facilities but often just as comfortable, from one star to three. A *hotel residencia* or *hostal residencia* is one that does not serve evening meals.

### BORN (€€)

Two-star *hotel residencia* in a converted mansion near the Born. Good value if you want character in the old city.

✉ Carrer Sant Jaume 3
☎ 971 712942;
www.hotelborn.com ⏰ All year

### CUITAT JARDI (€€€)

One of Mallorca's earliest tourist hotels, reopened after major renovation. The Moorish-style building is behind the beach, with fabulous views of Palma, a 1-hour walk around the bay.

✉ Carrer Illa de Malta 14, Cuitat Jardi ☎ 971 260007;
www.hcuitatie.com ⏰ All year

### DALT MURADA (€€)

Just eight elegant rooms furnished with antiques in a restored Gothic manor house near the cathedral.

✉ Carrer Almudaina 6A
☎ 971 425300 ⏰ All year

### MELIÁ VICTORIA (€€€)

Huge modern hotel which dominates the harbour. Most rooms have views of the cathedral and bay.

✉ Avinguda Joan Miró 21
☎ 971 732542;
www.solmelia.com ⏰ All year

### PALACIO CA SA GALESA (€€€)

A beautifully restored 17th-century merchant's house between the cathedral and the Arab baths. There is a rooftop terrace and the only indoor pool to be found in the old city.

✉ Carrer de Miramar 8
☎ 971 715400;
www.palaciocasagalesa.com ⏰ All year

### PALAU SA FONT (€€€)

A 16th-century palace converted into a boutique hotel, with pink walls, wooden floors and a small terrace pool.

✉ Carrer dels Apuntadors 38
☎ 971 712277; www.paulausafont.com ⏰ All year

### PORTIXOL (€€€)

Scandinavian design meets 1950s architecture in this seaside hotel in an up-and-coming harbour area.

✉ Carrer Sirena 27 ☎ 971 271800; www.portixol.com ⏰ All year

### PURO (€€€)

Ethnic bohemian chic at Palma's latest boutique hotel, which opened in 2004 in a restored mansion close to La Llotja.

✉ Carrer Montenegro 12
☎ 971 425450;
www.purohotel.com ⏰ All year

### RITZI (€)

Budget *hostal* centrally located for Palma's *tapas* bars and nightlife quarter.

✉ Carrer Apuntadors 6
☎ 971 714610 ⏰ All year

### SAN LORENZO (€€€)

Six rooms only in a restored 17th-century manor house. Attractive garden with swimming pool close to the old city.

✉ Carrer Sant Llorenç 14
☎ 971 728200; www.sanlorenzo.com ⏰ All year

### SON VIDA (€€€)

Exclusive hotel in a 13th-century castle with its own golf course.

✉ Urbanización Son Vida Raixa 2 ☎ 971 790000;
www.hotelsonvida.com ⏰ All year

# Around the Island

## ALCÚDIA

### ES CONVENT (€€€)
Four tastefully decorated rooms in a pair of stone houses in the heart of the old town.
✉ Carrer Progrès 6 ☎ 971 548716; www.esconvent.com
🕐 Feb–Nov

## ALGAIDA

### RAIMS (€€)
Rural apartments around the courtyard of a 17th-century manor house. Breakfast is taken in the delightful garden.
✉ Carrer Ribera 21 ☎ 971 665157; www.finca-raims.com
🕐 All year

## ARTÀ

### CA'N MORAGUES (€€)
Just eight rooms and a heated swimming pool and sauna in this stylish renovated town house.
✉ Carrer Pou Nou 12 ☎ 971 829509; www.canmoragues.com
🕐 All year

## BANYALBUFAR

### MAR I VENT (€€)
Wonderful views from the terrace of this family-run hotel. Swimming pool and tennis court.
✉ Carrer Major 49
☎ 971 618000 🕐 Feb–Nov

## BINISSALEM

### SCOTT'S TOWNHOUSE HOTEL (€€€)
Discreet hotel in a 19th-century town house – with all antique furniture and Persian rugs – on the church square.
✉ Plaça Església 12 ☎ 971 870100; www.scottshotel.com
🕐 All year

## CALA FIGUERA

### VILLA SERENA (€)
A simple two-star hotel well-positioned at the mouth of a pretty bay.
✉ Carrer Virgen del Carmen 37
☎ 971 645303 🕐 Apr–Oct

## CALA RAJADA

### SES ROTGES (€€)
An old-style villa with a beautiful flower-filled garden and a Michelin-starred restaurant.
✉ Carrer Rafael Blanes 21
☎ 971 563108 🕐 Apr–Oct

## DEIÀ

### LA RESIDENCIA (€€€)
A pair of 16th-century *fincas* with terraced orchards converted into a luxury hotel. Four-poster beds in every suite.
✉ Camí Son Canals ☎ 971 639011; www.hotel-laresidencia.com 🕐 Feb–Nov

### S'HOTEL D'ES PUIG (€€)
The 'hotel on the hill' as featured in a short story by Robert Graves and in Gordon West's *Jogging Round Majorca*.
✉ Carrer Es Puig 4
☎ 971 639409 🕐 All year

## FORMENTOR

### HOTEL FORMENTOR (€€€)
A grand hotel in a lovely setting between the beach and the pine woods, with acres of terraced gardens.
✉ Platja de Formentor
☎ 971 899100; www. hotelformentor.net 🕐 Apr–Oct

### REIS DE MALLORCA

Reis de Mallorca (Kings of Mallorca) is an independent group of 30 Mallorcan hotels. It includes some of the top hotels on the island, like Palacio Ca Sa Galesa in Palma, L'Hermitage in Orient and Illa d'Or in Port de Pollença, but also cheaper options like the Mar i Vent in Banyalbufar. What they all have in common is individuality, architectural beauty and generally excellent cuisine. Reis de Mallorca hotels can be booked on ☎ 971 770737 or visit www.reisdemallorca.com

# Around the Island

## MONASTERIES

Several of Mallorca's former monasteries rent out old monks' and pilgrims' cells to travellers. You may not get a shower but you will find peace, a sense of history and unforgettable hilltop views. The best known, at Lluc, is now virtually a hotel; for real solitude head instead for the Ermita de Bonany (➤ 52), Puig de Maria or the sanctuary above Castell d'Alaró (➤ 28).

### FORNALUTX

**CA'N VERDERA (€€€)**
An old stone house has been tastefully converted into a modern boutique hotel: relax among the orange groves.
✉ Carrer de Toros 1 ☎ 971 638203; www.canverdera.com
⏰ All year

### GALILEA

**SCOTT'S GALILEA (€€€)**
Newly opened sister establishment to Scott's Townhouse, some twenty minutes west of Palma. Three houses and seven studios in an attractive setting, self-catering, with breakfast included. Ideal for relaxation.
✉ Sa Costa Den Mandons 3 ☎ 971 870100; www.scottsgalilea.com ⏰ All year

### LLUC

**MONESTIR DE LLUC (€)**
Comfortable rooms in a former monastery – a good base for walking in the Serra de Tramuntana.
✉ Lluc monastery
☎ 971 871525 ⏰ All year

### LLUC-ALCARI

**COSTA D'OR (€€)**
Simple hotel in a magical setting above the sea; you can walk to the shore through the hotel's own pine forest.
✉ Lluc-Alcari ☎ 971 639025 ⏰ Apr–Oct

### MANACOR

**LA RESERVA ROTANA (€€€)**
This 17th-century mansion with its own golf course is typical of Mallorca's new breed of upmarket rural hotels.
✉ Cami de S'Avall, km3
☎ 971 845685 ⏰ Feb–Nov

### ORIENT

**DALT MUNTANYA (€€)**
A former walkers' hostel recently renovated as part of the trend towards upmarket rural tourism.
✉ Carretera de Bunyola
☎ 971 615373 ⏰ Feb–Oct

**L'HERMITAGE (€€€)**
A former convent turned into a country-house hotel, with swimming pool, tennis courts, sauna and a first-class restaurant.
✉ Carretera Alaró–Bunyola
☎ 971 180303; www.hermitage-hotel.com
⏰ Feb–Nov

### POLLENÇA

**JUMA (€€)**
This early 20th-century hotel on the main square has reopened its doors to cater for the growing numbers of people wanting to stay in inland towns. 8 comfortable rooms.
✉ Plaça Major 9 ☎ 971 535002; www.hoteljuma.com
⏰ All year

### PORT D' ANDRATX

**BRISMAR (€€)**
Centrally located on the seafront. Pleasant rooms with balcony overlooking the harbor.
✉ Carrer Almirante Riera Alemany 6 ☎ 971 671600; www.fehm.es/pma/brismar
⏰ Closed Dec, Jan

## PORT DE POLLENÇA

### ILLA D'OR (€€€)
Charming old-fashioned beach hotel at the end of the promenade.
✉ Passeig Colón 265
☎ 971 865100;
www.hoposa.es ◷ Feb–Nov

## PORT DE SÓLLER

### ES PORT (€€)
Three-star family-run *hostal* in a 15th-century mansion.
✉ Carrer Antoni Montis
☎ 971 631650; www.hotelsport.com ◷ Feb–Nov

## PUIGPUNYENT

### GRAN HOTEL SON NET (€€€)
Elegantly restored 17th-century mansion with swimming pool set in extensive grounds.
✉ Carrer Castillo de Sonnet s/n
☎ 971 147000; www.sonnet.es
◷ All year

## SANT ELM

### HOSTAL DRAGONERA (€)
Simple beach hotel with a sun terrace right by the sea. The hotel can arrange bike hire, walks and horse-riding.
✉ Avinguda Rei Jaume I 5
☎ 971 239086 ◷ Feb–Nov

## SANTA MARIA DEL CAMÌ

### READ'S (€€€)
British-run hotel and fine restaurant in a magnificent restored *finca*.
✉ Carretera Santa Maria–Alaró
☎ 971 140261 ◷ All year

## SES ILLETES

### BON SOL (€€€)
Delightful family-run hotel, arranged like a wedding-cake on several levels and cascading down a hill to its private beach.
✉ Passeig Illetes 30 ☎ 971 402111 ◷ Closed Nov

## SINEU

### SON CLEDA (€€)
Attractive three-star hotel in a restored 17th-century house overlooking the market square.
✉ Plaça Es Fossar 7 ☎ 971 521040 ◷ All year

## SÓLLER

### CA N'AI (€€€)
Four-star *hotel rural* in a manor house surrounded by orange groves.
✉ Camì Son Sales 50
☎ 971 632494 ◷ Feb–Oct

### EL GUÍA (€€)
Excellent value old-style hotel/restaurant near the station.
✉ Carrer Castanyer 2
☎ 971 630227 ◷ Apr–Oct

## VALLDEMOSSA

### CA'N MARIO (€)
Charming family-run *hostal* filled with antiques. Good first-floor restaurant.
✉ Carrer Uetam 8 ☎ 971 612122 ◷ Closed Jan

### VALLDEMOSSA (£££)
Luxury hotel with a celebrated restaurant in a restored *finca* with its own orchards and gardens.
✉ Carretera Vieja de Valldemossa ☎ 971 612626
◷ All year

### FINCAS

Many of Mallorca's *fincas* (country estates) have recently been converted into upmarket tourist accommodation, combining character (stone farmhouses, antiques and beautiful views) with modern amenities like swimming pools. You can get information on *fincas* from the Associació Agroturisme Balear, Avinguda Gabriel Alomar Villalonga 8a, Palma (☎ 971 721508; www.topfincas.com) or from the independent association (www.fincaturismo.com).

# Markets

## WEEKLY MARKETS

Almost every town in Mallorca has a weekly market; most start early and wind up by lunchtime. The larger markets all follow a similar pattern – fresh produce around the main square, specialist food stalls fanning out from there, then cheap clothes, household goods and craft stalls for the tourists. The biggest market is on Thursdays at Inca; the most traditional is the Wednesday agricultural and livestock market at Sineu.

### PALMA

#### LLOTJA DEL PEIX (FISH MARKET)

Get here early as the night's catch goes on sale and mullet, prawns, sardines and sea bass are hawked by women with operatic voices.

- ✉ Es Moll de Pescadors
- ☎ 971 721182
- ◷ Mon–Sat 6am

#### MERCAT ARTESANAL

This lively craft market on the Plaça Major also features buskers and open-air cafés.

- ✉ Plaça Major  ◷ Mon–Sat 10–8 in summer; Fri, Sat only in winter

#### MERCAT OLIVAR

Palma's main market, in a hall near Plaça d'Espanya. Meat, fish and fresh produce on the ground floor, and a supermarket upstairs. Huge piles of oranges and tomatoes, buckets full of olives, meat and cheese counters and fresh fish stalls.

- ✉ Plaça Olivar  ☎ 971 720315  ◷ Mon–Sat 7–2

#### RAMBLA

It may not match its Barcelona namesake, but Palma's Rambla is similar, lined with flower stalls.

- ✉ Passeig de la Rambla
- ◷ Mon–Fri 8–2, 5–8, Sat 8–2

#### RASTRO (FLEA MARKET)

A Palma institution which takes over part of the main ring road each Saturday morning. Plenty of bargains but lots of junk too.

- ✉ Avinguda de Gabriel Alomar i Villalonga  ◷ Sat 8–2

### SANTA CATALINA

Fresh fruit and vegetable market just west of the city centre, in the district of the same name. This is where some of Palma's top chefs come to do their shopping. As well as fresh produce, meat and fish, the market also has delicatesen stalls specialising in wine, oils, vinegars and sushi.

- ✉ Plaça Navegació  ☎ 971 730710  ◷ Mon–Sat 8–2

### OUTSIDE PALMA

Alaró – *Sat*
Alcúdia – *Tue, Sun*
Algaida – *Fri*
Andratx – *Wed*
Artà – *Tue*
Binissalem – *Fri*
Cala Rajada – *Sat*
Calvià – *Mon*
Campos – *Thu, Sat*
Capdepera – *Wed*
Colònia de Sant Jordi – *Wed*
Felanitx – *Sun*
Inca – *Thu*
Llucmajor – *Wed, Sun*
Manacor – *Mon*
Montuïri – *Mon*
Muro – *Sun*
Petra – *Wed*
Pollença – *Sun*
Porreres – *Tue*
Port de Pollença – *Wed*
Porto Cristo – *Sun*
Pòrtol – *Thu*
Santa Eugènia – *Sat*
Santa Maria del Camí – *Sun*
Santanyí – *Wed, Sat*
S'Arenal – *Thu*
Ses Salines – *Thu*
Sineu – *Wed*
Sóller – *Sat*
Valldemossa – *Sun*
Vilafranca de Bonany – *Wed*

# Shopping in Palma

## SHOPPING DISTRICTS

The main shopping areas in Palma are Avinguda Jaume III for upmarket boutiques and the pedestrian streets around Plaça Major for small specialist shops. Centro Comercial Porto Pi, a modern shopping mall and hypermarket complex, is 2km from the centre.

## BOOKS

### LA CASA DEL MAPA
Books and maps about Mallorca.
✉ Carrer Sant Domingo 11
☎ 971 225944

### ERESO
Good selection of books about Mallorca in English and German.
✉ Carrer Paraires 1
☎ 971 710283

### FIOL
Palma's leading second-hand bookshop.
✉ Carrer Oms 45
☎ 971 721428

### FUNDACIÓ LA CAIXA
Art books and posters on the ground floor of this modern art gallery.
✉ Plaça Weyler 3 ☎ 971 728071 ⏱ Mon–Sat 10–9, Sun 10–2

## DEPARTMENT STORES

### EL CORTE INGLÉS
Mallorca's two branches of Spain's leading department store. The Club del Gourmet has Spanish wines, hams and cheeses.

✉ Avinguda Jaume III 15; Avinguda Alexandre Rosselló 12
☎ 971 770177
⏱ Mon–Sat 9.30–9.30

## FOOD & WINE

### BONS VINS
Excellent selection of Mallorcan and Spanish wines and olive oils.
✉ Carrer Sant Feliu 7
☎ 971 214041

### COLMADO SANTO DOMINGO
Hundreds of hanging *sobrasada* sausages and cheeses, fig cake and oils.
✉ Carrer Sant Domingo 1
☎ 971 714887

### FORN D'ES TEATRE
Art nouveau shopfront, and a good place to buy *ensaimadas*.
✉ Plaça Weyler 9
☎ 971 715254

### FORN FONDO
This bakery has been turning out *ensaimadas* since 1911.
✉ Carrer Unió 15
☎ 971 711634

### FRASQUET
Go in here just to smell the melted chocolate.
✉ Carrer Brossa 19
☎ 971 721354

### LA MONTAÑA
Sausages, hams, cheeses and one of Palma's best window displays.
✉ Carrer Jaume II 27
☎ 971 712595

### SON VIVOT
Mallorcan and Menorcan produce.
✉ Plaça Porta Pintada 1
☎ 971 720748

## SHOPPING TIPS

Most shops are open from around 10 to 1.30 and 5 to 8 Monday to Friday, and on Saturday mornings. The exceptions are souvenir shops in the large resorts, which stay open every day, and larger supermarkets open throughout the day Monday to Saturday. Most shops accept credit cards, but it is always advisable to have some cash.

# Arts and Crafts in Palma

### SIURELLS

*Siurells* are clay whistles, which have been made on Mallorca since Arab times. They come in all shapes and sizes – the most common design is a man on horseback – and are painted white with flashes of red and green. They are cheap, children love them, and the artist Joan Miró was much influenced by their brightness and simplicity.

### ALPARGATERÍA LLINAS
The best place to buy espadrilles.
✉ Carrer Sant Miquel 43
☎ 971 717696

### CAMPER
Camper shoes are both funky and functional and this Mallorcan firm has become a global brand. There are other branches on Avingunda Jaume III, at Porto Pí and at the airport, as well as factory outlet stores at Inca and Festival Park (▶ facing page).
✉ Carrer Sant Miquel 17
☎ 971 726254

### LA CASA DEL OLIVO
Wonderful olive-carver's workshop in an alley off Carrer Jaume II. The best buy here is salad bowls – they're not cheap but you're paying for the quality and old-fashioned craftsmanship.
✉ Carrer Pescateria Vella 4
☎ 971 727025

### FANG I FOC
This shop stocks a good range of ceramics from Mallorca and the Spanish mainland.
✉ Carrer Libertat 29
☎ 971 455860

### FET A MÀ
As the name implies, everything is 'made by hand'. Pottery and glass are on sale, in traditional and modern style.
✉ Carrer Sant Miquel 52
☎ 971 711095

### HERREROS DE VICENTE JUAN RIBAS
The best place in Palma to buy *roba de llengues* patterned cloth.

✉ Carrer Sant Nicolau 10
☎ 971 721773

### MAJÓRICA
Palma branch of Mallorca's leading artificial-pearl-maker.
✉ Avingunda Jaume III 11
☎ 971 725268/722919

### MIDGE DALTON
Palma's antique shops are perfect for browsing, and this is one of the best.
✉ Plaça Mercat 20
☎ 971 713360

### NATURA
Palma's branch of Natura selling eco-friendly gifts.
✉ Passeig des Born 9
☎ 971 718252

### PASSEIG PER L'ARTESANIA
A complex of craft shops and workshops set in an old factory, where artists sell woodwork, pottery, glassware, paperwork, recycled goods, food and wine – all made in Mallorca.
✉ Plaça Llorenç Bisbal Batle
☎ 971 717717

### PERSÉPOLIS
High-class antiques on Palma's upmarket shopping street.
✉ Avingunda Jaume III 23
☎ 971 724539

### S'AVARCA
Traditional Menorcan handmade sandals.
✉ Carrer Sant Domingo 14
☎ 971 712058

### VIDRIERÍAS GORDIOLA
The best choice of Algaida glassware in Palma.
✉ Carrer Victoria 6
☎ 971 711541

# Arts and Crafts Around the Island

## ALGAIDA

**VIDRIOS GORDIOLA**
Glass factory and museum
(► 59) in a mock castle.
✉ Carretera Palma–Manacor,
km19 ☎ 971 665046

## FELANITX

**CERAMIQUES FELANITX**
A large selection of local
pottery at competitive
prices.
✉ Carrer Major 12
☎ 971 580395

## INCA

**MUNPER**
Mallorcan leather is rarely
a bargain, but come here
for a wide selection of
shoes, handbags and belts.
✉ Carretera Palma–Alcúdia,
km30 ☎ 971 881000

## MANACOR

**MAJÓRICA**
Shop here after touring
Mallorca's largest pearl
factory (► 59).
✉ Avinguda Majórica 48
☎ 971 550200

**OLIVART**
Everything here is made
from olive wood.
✉ Carretera Palma–Manacor,
km45 ☎ 971 552800

## MONTUÏRI

**ORQUÍDEA**
Large factory shop
featuring artificial pearls.
✉ Carretera Palma–Manacor,
km30 ☎ 971 644144

## PÒRTOL

**CA MADÒ BET**
Hand-made *siurells*
(► panel 76) produced in
a village house .
✉ Carrer Jaume I 10, Sa
Cabeneta ☎ 971 602497

**CA'S CANONGE**
Large selection of pottery,
especially heavy brown-
glazed cooking pots.
✉ Carrer Ca's Canonge 41
☎ 971 602361

**ROCA LLISA**
One of the best places to
buy *siurells* (► panel 76).
✉ Carrer Roca Llisa 24
☎ 971 602497

## SANTA MARIA DEL CAMÍ

**CA'N BERNAT**
Master craftsman's
workshop turning out
imaginative local pottery.
✉ Carrer Bartomeu Pasqual
☎ 971 621306

## SANTANYÍ

**CERÀMIQUES DE SANTANYÍ**
Innovative ceramic
designs, based on ancient
Mallorcan traditions.
✉ Carrer Guardia Civil 22
☎ 971 163128

## SÓLLER

**EUGENIO**
Gifts carved out of olive
wood – salad bowls, salt-
cellars, chess sets.
✉ Carrer Jerónimo Estades
11A ☎ 971 630984

**FET A SÓLLER**
Shop in the station selling
local produce and crafts.
Profits go to a workshop
for those with disabilities.
✉ Estació de Sóller
☎ 971 633942

### CRAFT FAIRS

A *Fira del Fang* (Ceramics
Fair) is held each March in the
town of Marratxí and all of
Mallorca's leading potters are
represented. Prices here are
much better than in the tourist
shops. *Baleart* is a Christmas
craft fair held in Palma each
December, with stalls selling
everything from pottery and
handmade shoes to Mallorcan
wines and *sobrasada*
sausages.

### FACTORY OUTLETS

There are numerous factory
shops selling leather, pearls
and glassware on the main
roads across the island. One of
the best is RECamper, an
outlet store for Camper shoes
in a warehouse off the Inca
bypass. Camper also have an
outlet store at Festival Park, an
American-style mall off the
Palma-Inca motorway, with
fast-food restaurants, cinemas
and the Green Planet
reptilarium.

# Theatres and Concerts

## WHAT'S ON?

To find out what's on while you are staying, ask any tourist office for a copy of *Where To Go*, published quarterly in English and German. The *Majorca Daily Bulletin* also has daily listings. A monthly guide to events in Palma is published in Spanish and Catalan and available at tourist offices and hotels. Remember that everything starts late in Mallorca – opera at 9pm, theatre around 10pm and music any time up to midnight.

## COSTA NORD

The American actor Michael Douglas could be seen as a 21st-century successor to Archduke Ludwig Salvator, using his money and his influence to promote the landscapes and culture of Mallorca. In 2000 he opened Costa Nord, a multimedia cultural centre in Valldemossa devoted to Mallorca's north coast. The visit begins with a short film, narrated by Douglas; it continues with a recreation of the Archduke's yacht, the *Nixe*, accompanied by a commentary on his Mediterranean voyages. The shop sells a range of pricey souvenirs; there is also a concert hall which attracts top international names during the Mediterranean Nights festival each summer.
✉ Avinguda Palma 6
☎ 971 612425

## PALMA

### AUDITÒRIUM
This is Palma's main venue for theatre and concerts.
✉ Passeig Marítim 18
☎ 971 734735

### CASTELL DE BELLVER
Popular venue for outdoor classical concerts on balmy summer evenings.
✉ Parc Bellver
☎ 971 730657

### PARC DE LA MAR
Free concerts (jazz, rock or classical) beneath the city walls in summer.
✉ Parc de la Mar

### TEATRE MUNICIPAL
Contemporary drama, dance and ballet are all staged here, as well as film screenings.
✉ Passeig Mallorca 9
☎ 971 739148

### TEATRE SANS
Cutting-edge drama in Catalan at back-street fringe theatre.
✉ Carrer Ca'n Sanç 5
☎ 971 727266

### TEATRE XESC FORTEZA
The place for contemporary drama and music in a new theatre, which opened in 2003.
✉ Plaça Prevere Miquel Maura 1 ☎ 971 720135

## ALCÚDIA

### AUDITORI D'ALCÚDIA
A stunning new hall hosting concerts and drama.
✉ Plaça de la Porta de Mallorca
☎ 971 897185

## CALA MILLOR

### SA MÀNIGA
New auditorium with regular concerts and exhibitions.
✉ Carrer Son Galta 4
☎ 971 587373

## DEIÀ

### SON MARROIG
Concerts are staged on summer evenings in the gardens created by Archduke Ludwig Salvator. Deià's annual classical music festival is held here.
✉ Carretera Valldemossa–Deià ☎ 971 639158

## ESPORLES

### LA GRANJA
Displays of folk music and dancing on Wednesday and Friday afternoons.
✉ La Granja
☎ 971 610032

## POLLENÇA

### CONVENT SANT DOMINGO
Pollença's annual music festival is held in the cloisters of this 17th-century monastery.
✉ Carrer Sant Domingo
☎ 971 531008

## VALLDEMOSSA

### REIAL CARTOIXA
The Chopin festival is held each August in the town's Carthusian monastery. Internationally renowned musicians play works by Chopin and other leading composers.
✉ Valldemossa
☎ 971 612106

# Bars

## RESORT BARS

Bars in the main resorts change their names and identities so frequently that recommendations are useless – follow your nose and you will soon find one that you like. Many bars are foreign-owned, with German or British names, imported beer and satellite TV. A stretch of the Platja de Palma is known as *carrer de la cervesa* ('Beer Street') owing to the number of German bars; the British equivalent is in Magaluf.

## PALMA

The best places for late-night bar-hopping are in the streets around Plaça de la Llotja and the terrace bars along the waterfront on Passeig Marítim.

### BARCELONA

Cool jazz bar in a basement beside Abaco.
✉ Carrer Apuntadors 5
☎ 971 713557  🕐 9pm; live jazz nightly from midnight

### CAPPUCCINO GRAND CAFÉ

The hippest meeting place in town in an old Renaissance palace with a courtyard and art gallery.
✉ Carrer San Miquel 53
☎ 971 719764  🕐 8am–1am

### CAPPUCCINO GRAND CAFÉ

The original Café, on the waterfront, is still a popular place to meet for coffee or cocktails.
✉ Passeig Marítim 1
☎ 971 282162
🕐 8.30am–3am

### DÀRSENA

For an up-to-the-minute buzz, try this fashionable waterfront terrace bar with a great location by the harbour.
✉ Passeig Marítim  ☎ 971 180504  🕐 Mon–Sat 8am–midnight, Sun 8am–9pm

### HOGANS

Palma's first Irish pub opened in 1996. Occasional Irish fiddling, popular with locals.
✉ Carrer Monsenyor Palmer 2
☎ 971 289664
🕐 12 noon–3am

### EL PESQUERO

Former fishermen's bar, now a chic waterfront café with *tapas*, drinks and harbour views.
✉ Moll de la Llotja 2  ☎ 971 715220  🕐 10am–late

### VARADERO

Trendy terrace bar at the end of the old quay, with great views of the floodlit cathedral.
✉ Moll Vell  ☎ 971 726428
🕐 9am–late

## NEAR PALMA

### ABACANTO

A cousin of Abaco (see panel) in a 19th-century mansion in the suburb of S'Indioteria. It is quite difficult to find, so take a taxi.
✉ Camí Son Nicolau, S'Indioteria  ☎ 971 430624
🕐 9pm–2am

### HAVANA MOON

The trendiest of many bars by the ritzy Puerto Portals marina.
✉ Puerto Portals  ☎ 971 677522  🕐 5pm–4am

### ABACO

Palma's most unusual bar is located in a 17th-century palace close to La Llotja. Push open a heavy wooden door in the busy nightlife quarter and you enter a different world. Huge baskets of fruit cascade onto the floor; there are fresh flowers everywhere, and a subtle hint of incense. You sip fruit cocktails by candlelight, while listening to classical music, then wander into the courtyard with its fountains and caged birds. The drinks are expensive, but everyone should go once.
✉ Carrer Sant Joan 1
☎ 971 715974  🕐 8am–3am

# Discos and Dinner Shows

## DINNER SHOWS

A recent arrival in Mallorca is the 'themed' dinner show and spectacle, which can be anything from folklore and flamenco dancing to a medieval banquet complete with jousting and serving wenches. These shows are basically aimed at tour groups; you can book at any resort hotel. Don't go unless you are prepared to abandon your inhibitions and join in the fun.

## DISCOS

### PALMA

#### MAR SALADA
Cool late-night disco right on the harbour, within the Club de Mar.
- ✉ Moll de Pelaires
- ☎ 971 702709
- ⏰ Fri–Sat 11pm–6am

#### PACHA
A branch of one of the most famous club chains, Pacha is for those in search of a serious night out.
- ✉ Passeig Marítim 42
- ☎ 971 737788 ⏰ 11pm–6am; nightly in summer; Thu–Sat in winter

#### TITO'S
Not quite as young as nearby Pacha (▶ above). There are six bars, a laser show and fantastic views over Palma bay. To get in you enter via an outdoor lift from the seafront promenade.
- ✉ Passeig Marítim
- ☎ 971 730017
- ⏰ 11pm–6am; Tue–Sun; Thu–Sat in winter

### AROUND THE ISLAND

#### BCM
This is the largest and probably the loudest disco in Europe, with laser shows, banks of video screens, a swimming pool and room for 4,000 people. The upper level is dedicated to the young-and-trendy crowd, while the over-30s gather downstairs. Big-name international stars are featured in live shows here throughout the summer season.
- ✉ Avinguda S'Olivera, Magaluf ☎ 971 131546
- ⏰ 10pm–5am; nightly in summer, weekends in winter

#### MENTA
Designed like a Roman temple around an open-air pool, it honours Alcúdia's history each May with a 'Roman orgy'.
- ✉ Avinguda Tucan, Port d'Alcúdia ☎ 971 891972
- ⏰ 11pm–6am, nightly in summer; weekends in winter

#### RIU PALACE
Large, loud international disco club with visits from top European DJs in summer.
- ✉ Las Maravillas ☎ 971 743474 ⏰ 11pm–6am, nightly in summer

## DINNER SHOWS

### AROUND THE ISLAND

#### CASINO MALLORCA
A choice of gambling in the casino (passport and smart dress required) or the Paladium dinner show with dancing.
- ✉ Urbanización Sol de Mallorca, Magaluf ☎ 971 130000 ⏰ Casino Mon–Sat 6pm–4am, Sun 3pm–4am

#### PIRATE ADVENTURE
Yo-ho-ho and a bundle of fun on a mock pirate ship – with plenty of audience participation required. Don't say you weren't warned!
- ✉ Carretera La Porrassa, Magaluf ☎ 971 130411
- ⏰ May–Oct, Mon–Fri (times vary)

# Golf Courses

## PALMA

**SON VIDA**
Get out of town to
Mallorca's first golf course,
opened in 1964 on an
exclusive estate above
Palma.
✉ Urbanización Son Vida
☎ 971 791210

## BUNYOLA

**SON TERMENS**
Attractive course on an old
hunting estate.
✉ Carrer de S'Esglaieta, km10
☎ 971 617862

## CALA MILLOR

**SON SERVERA**
Nine-hole course amid
pine woods by the sea.
✉ Urbanización Costa dels
Pins, 6km from Cala Millor
☎ 971 840096

## CAMP DE MAR

**GOLF DE ANDRATX**
A challenging course with
narrow fairways, lakes and
sea views.
✉ Carretera Camp de Mar
☎ 971 236280

## CAPDEPERA

**CANYAMEL**
A testing course – small
greens, sloping fairways
and sea breezes.
✉ Urbanización Canyamel
☎ 971 841313

**PULA GOLF**
Take on this challenging
course on a luxury resort
between Cala Millor and
Capdepera.
✉ Carretera Son Servera–
Capdepera, km3 ☎ 971
817034

## LLUCMAJOR

**SON ANTEM ESTE**
Wide fairways, fast greens
and hidden water hazards.
A second course, Son
Antem Oeste, opened in
2001.
✉ 3km outside Llucmajor on
the PM602 to Palma
☎ 971 129200

## MAGALUF

**PONIENTE**
A long, difficult 18-holes.
✉ Carretera Cala Figuera
☎ 971 130148

## POLLENÇA

**POLLENÇA**
Tight 9-hole course, with
small greens and narrow
fairways with sea views.
✉ 2km outside Pollença on
Palma road ☎ 971 533216

## PORTO COLOM

**VALL D'OR**
Set among pine trees close
to the east coast.
✉ Carretera Porto Colom–Cala
d'Or ☎ 971 837068

## SANTA PONÇA

**SANTA PONÇA**
Venue for the Balearic
Open: long, wide fairways
set in open countryside.
✉ Urbanización Golf Santa
Ponça ☎ 971 690211

## SES ILLETES

**REAL GOLF DE
BENDINAT**
Undulating course set
among pine woods above
the bay of Palma.
✉ Urbanización Bendinat
☎ 971 405200

**GOLF IN MALLORCA**

In 1976 there were two golf
courses in Mallorca; now there
are no less than 20 spread
over the island. All are open
throughout the year, providing
a refuge for golfers fleeing
frost and winter greens
elsewhere. The typical cost of
a round is €60–€70, though
this is much reduced if you
come on a golfing package
holiday. Don't forget to bring a
handicap certificate.

**LATEST COURSE**
Mallorca's newest golf course
opened in 2003 in a stunning
setting at Alcanada on the
Victòria peninsula .
✉ Carretera del Faro
☎ 971 549560.

# Watersports

## SAILING IN MALLORCA

Mallorca has some 43 marinas, 30 sailing clubs and moorings for over 10,000 boats. Yachts can be chartered locally and most marinas also have facilities for water-skiing and windsurfing. Highlights of the sailing year include the King's Cup in August, the Princess Sofía trophy at Easter, and the Rei en Jaume regatta in July when a flotilla of yachts re-creates the 185km journey made by Jaume the Conqueror when he landed at Santa Ponça in 1229.

## WINDSURFING

There are schools at several of the larger resorts and it is also possible to hire equipment without tuition. Beaches where windsurfing is available include Cala Millor, Cala d'Or, Can Picafort, Formentor, Magaluf, Palma Nova, Peguera, Platja de Palma, Port d'Alcúdia, Port de Pollença, Port de Sóller, Portals Nous and Santa Ponça.

## SAILING

### ESCUELA NACIONAL DE VELA CALANOVA

The national sailing school in Cala Major runs courses and is also willing to offer advice on all aspects of sailing in and around the sea off Mallorca.

✉ Avinguda Joan Miró, Cala Major ☎ 971 402512

### SAIL AND SURF POLLENÇA

This prestigious sailing club and school is located on the northeast coast. Instruction is available both for beginners and for those more experienced.

✉ Passeig Saralegui 134, Port de Pollença ☎ 971 865346

### ALCÚDIAMAR, PORT D'ALCÚDIA MARINA
☎ 971 546000

### CALA D'OR MARINA
☎ 971 657070

### CLUB DE MAR, PALMA
☎ 971 403611

### PORT D'ANDRATX MARINA
☎ 971 671721

### PORT DE POLLENÇA MARINA
☎ 971 864635

### PORT DE SÓLLER MARINA
☎ 971 633316

### PORTO COLOM MARINA
☎ 971 824658

### PORTO CRISTO MARINA
☎ 971 821253

### PUERTO PORTALS MARINA (PORTALS NOUS)
☎ 971 171100

## SCUBA DIVING
### FEDERACIÓ BALEAR DE ACTIVIDADES SUBACUÁTICAS

The clear waters around the island of Mallorca are the perfect place for diving, especially in the small, shallow coves of the south and east coasts. The federation can give you information and advice on all aspects of diving, therefore, it is a good starting point.

✉ Polideportivo San Moix, Palma ☎ 971 288242

### ALBATROS
✉ Port Cala Bona, Cala Millor
☎ 971 586807

### AQUA MARINE DIVING
✉ Port d'Andratx
☎ 971 674376

### EL BUCEO
✉ Port d'Andratx
☎ 971 674217

### OCTOPUS
✉ Port de Sóller
☎ 971 633133

### SCUBA ACTIVA
✉ Sant Elm
☎ 971 239102

## WATER-SKIING

Water-skiing equipment can be hired on all the most popular beaches, including Cala Millor, Can Picafort, Magaluf, Palma Nova, Peguera, Platja de Palma, Port d'Alcúdia and Santa Ponça.

# Spectator Sports

## BULLFIGHTING

Bullfighting is considered an art form as much as a sport – a legacy from pagan rites. The leading *matadors* are national celebrities and there are fights most days on TV. A bullfight begins with a horseback procession, or *corrida*, followed by the fight itself; the bull is softened up by *picadores* and then the *matador* moves in for the kill. Many foreigners may detest the spectacle – but it is undoubtedly an important aspect of Spanish culture.

### PALMA

**PLAÇA DE TOROS**
Bullfights are held in this 1929 bullring between March and October. Choose between a seat in the sun (*sol*) or the shade (*sombra*).
✉ Avinguda Gaspar Bennazar Arquitecte ☎ 971 755245

### AROUND THE ISLAND

**PLAÇA DE TOROS, ALCÚDIA**
☎ 971 547903

**PLAÇA DE TOROS, FELANITX**
☎ 971 580557

**PLAÇA DE TOROS, INCA**
☎ 971 500087

**PLAÇA DE TOROS, MURO**
This bullring was built in 1910 inside its own quarry of white stone.
☎ 971 537 329

## CRICKET

### AROUND THE ISLAND

**MAGALUF CRICKET CLUB**
Cricket has been kept going by a group of British ex-patriates, who play local and visiting sides on their ground in Magaluf.
☎ 971 682880

## FOOTBALL

### PALMA

**SON MOIX**
The home of Real Mallorca FC, who play in the first division and reached the final of the European Cup Winners Cup in 1999. Matches on alternate Sunday afternoons, September to June.
✉ Camí dels Reis
☎ 971 221221

## HORSE-RACING

### PALMA

**HIPÓDROMO SON PARDO**
Europe's first floodlit racecourse opened in 1965. Trotting races (*carreras*) are held around a 1km track at 4.30 on Sundays in winter and 9pm on Fridays in summer. The jockey sits in a small cart behind the horse and must prevent the horse from breaking into a gallop. Trotting has been popular in Mallorca and Menorca for at least 200 years.
✉ Carretera Palma–Sóller, km3 ☎ 971 754031

*TIRO CON HONDA* (SLINGSHOT)
The Roman historian Livy wrote of Balearic slingshot throwers being employed as mercenaries during Hannibal's crossing of the Alps in 218 BC; a statue of a Balearic slinger in the S'Hort del Rei gardens in Palma is a tribute to their importance in Mallorcan history. The art of the slingshot has recently been revived; to see today's slingers, contact the Club de Honderos,
✉ Bar España, Carrer Oms 31, Palma ☎ 971 726250, or check out the website of the Federació Balear de Tir de Fona at www.tirdefona.com

**BALLOONING**
Mallorca Balloons offers trips in a hot-air balloon, with magnificent views of the whole island. Passengers are picked up and taken to Manacor for an early start.
✉ PO Box no. 11, 07590 Cala Rajada
☎ 971 565332/818182; www.mallorcaballoons.com

# MALLORCA
*practical matters*

### WHAT YOU NEED

| ● Required<br>○ Suggested<br>▲ Not required | Some countries require a passport to remain valid for a minimum period (usually at least six months) beyond the date of entry – contact their consulate or embassy or your travel agent for details. | UK | Germany | USA | Netherlands | Spain |
|---|---|---|---|---|---|---|
| Passport/National Identity Card | | ● | ● | ● | ● | ▲ |
| Visa (regulations can change – check before planning your journey) | | ▲ | ▲ | ▲ | ▲ | ▲ |
| Onward or Return Ticket | | ○ | ○ | ● | ○ | ○ |
| Health Inoculations | | ▲ | ▲ | ▲ | ▲ | ▲ |
| Health Documentation (➤ 90, Health) | | ● | ● | ● | ● | ▲ |
| Travel Insurance | | ○ | ○ | ○ | ○ | ○ |
| Driving Licence (non-EU nationals require an international driving licence) | | ● | ● | ● | ● | ● |
| Car Insurance Certificate | | ● | ● | ● | ● | ○ |
| Car Registration Document | | ● | ● | ● | ● | ○ |

### WHEN TO GO

**Palma**

High season

Low season

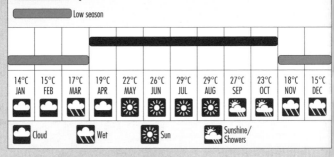

| 14°C<br>JAN | 15°C<br>FEB | 17°C<br>MAR | 19°C<br>APR | 22°C<br>MAY | 26°C<br>JUN | 29°C<br>JUL | 29°C<br>AUG | 27°C<br>SEP | 23°C<br>OCT | 18°C<br>NOV | 15°C<br>DEC |
|---|---|---|---|---|---|---|---|---|---|---|---|

Cloud    Wet    Sun    Sunshine/Showers

### TIME DIFFERENCES

| GMT<br>12 noon | Mallorca<br>1pm | Germany<br>1pm | USA (NY)<br>7am | Netherlands<br>1pm | Rest of Spain<br>1pm |
|---|---|---|---|---|---|

### TOURIST OFFICES

**In the UK**
Spanish Tourist Office
PO Box 4009
London W1A 6NB
☎ 020 7486 8077
Fax: 020 7486 8034
www.spain.info

**In the USA**
Tourist Office of Spain
35th Floor, 665 Fifth Avenue
New York
NY 10103
☎ 212/265 8822
Fax: 212/265 8864
www.okspain.org

Tourist Office of Spain
8383 Wilshire Boulevard
Suite 960
Beverly Hills
CA 90211
☎ 323/658 7188
Fax: 323/658 1061
www.okspain.org

## ARRIVING

Spain's national airline, Iberia, has scheduled flights to Palma's Son Sant Joan Airport from major Spanish and European cities, but charter flights are much cheaper. Ferry services operate from the Spanish mainland, Menorca and Ibiza to Palma.

**Son Sant Joan Airport**
Kilometres to city centre

**8 kilometres**

| Journey times | |
|---|---|
|  | N/A |
| | 30 minutes |
| | 15 minutes |

**Palma Ferry Terminal**
Kilometres to city centre

**2 kilometres**

| Journey times | |
|---|---|
| | N/A |
| | 30 minutes |
| | 10 minutes |

## MONEY

The euro is the official currency of Spain. Euro banknotes and coins were introduced in January 2002. Spain's former currency, the peseta, went out of circulation in early 2002.

Banknotes are in denominations of 5, 10, 20, 50, 100, 200 and 500 euros; coins are in denominations of 1, 2, 5, 10, 20 and 50 cents, and 1 and 2 euros.

Euro traveller's cheques are widely accepted, as are major credit cards. Credit and debit cards can also be used for withdrawing euro notes from ATMs. Banks can be found in most towns in Mallorca.

## TIME

 Like the rest of Spain, Mallorca is one hour ahead of Greenwich Mean Time (GMT+1), but from late March until late October, summer time (GMT+2) operates.

## CUSTOMS

 You may bring goods such as cigarettes and spirits into Mallorca, from an EU country, for personal use, within these guidelines:
800 cigarettes, 200 cigars, 1 kilogram of tobacco
10 litres of spirits (+22%)
20 litres of aperitifs
90 litres of wine, of which 60 litres can be sparkling wine
110 litres of beer

**If you are bringing goods into Mallorca from a non-EU country, for your personal use, the allowances are:**
200 cigarettes OR 50 cigars OR 250 grams of tobacco
1 litre of spirits (+22%)
2 litres of intermediary products (e.g. sherry) and sparkling wine
2 litres of still wine
50 grams of perfume
0.25 litres of eau de toilette
The value limit for goods is 175 euros.

**Travellers under 17 years of age are not entitled to the tobacco and alcohol allowance.**

**NO**
Drugs, firearms, ammunition, offensive weapons, obscene material, unlicensed animals.

## CONSULATES

UK
☎ 971 712445

Germany
☎ 971 707737

USA
☎ 971 403707

Netherlands
☎ 971 716493

## TOURIST OFFICES

**Local Tourist Offices
(Oficinas de Información
Turística – OIT)**

**Palma**
- Plaça de la Reina 2
  Palma 07012
  ☎ 971 712216

- Ca'n Solleric, Passeig des Born 27
  Palma 07001
  ☎ 971 724090

- Parc de les Estacions
  Palma 07002
  ☎ 971 754329

**Palma Nova**
- Passeig de la Mar 13
  Calvià 07181
  ☎ 971 682365

**Port d'Alcúdia**
- Passeig Marítim s/n
  Alcúdia 07410
  ☎ 971 547257

**Port de Pollença**
- Carrer de les Monges 9
  Pollença 07470
  ☎ 971 865467

**Sóller**
- Plaça d'Espanya s/n
  Sóller 07100
  ☎ 971 638008

Other offices include: Cala d'Or, Cala
Millor, Cala Rajada, Cala Sant Vicenç,
Ca'n Picafort, Colònia de Sant Jordi,
Magaluf, Peguera, Platja de Murro,
Port de Sóller, Porto Cristo, S'Arenal,
Ses Illetes, and Santa Ponça.

## NATIONAL HOLIDAYS

| J | F | M | A | M | J | J | A | S | O | N | D |
|---|---|---|---|---|---|---|---|---|---|---|---|
| 2 |   | (2) | (2) | 1 |   |   | 1 |   | 1 | 1 | 3 |

| | |
|---|---|
| 1 Jan | New Year's Day |
| 6 Jan | Epiphany |
| Mar/Apr | Good Friday, Easter Monday |
| 1 May | Labour Day |
| 15 Aug | Assumption of the Virgin |
| 12 Oct | National Day |
| 1 Nov | All Saints' Day |
| 6 Dec | Constitution Day |
| 8 Dec | Feast of the Immaculate Conception |
| 25 Dec | Christmas Day |

Many shops and offices close for longer periods around Christmas and
Easter, as well as for the festivals of Corpus Christi in May/June and
Sant Jaume on 25 July.

## OPENING HOURS

| ○ Shops | ● Churches |
|---|---|
| ● Offices | ◐ Museums |
| ● Banks | ◐ Pharmacies |

| 9 | 10 | 11 | 12 | 1 | 2 | 3 | 4 | 5 | 6 |
|---|---|---|---|---|---|---|---|---|---|
| am | am | am | am | pm | pm | pm | pm | pm | pm |
| 9.30 | 10.30 | 11.30 | 12.30 | 1.30 | 2.30 | 3.30 | 4.30 | 5.30 | |

In addition to the times shown above, large department stores, as well as
supermarkets and shops in tourist resorts, may open outside these times,
especially in summer. In general, pharmacies, banks and shops close on
Saturday afternoon, though banks stay open until 4.30PM Monday to
Thursday, October to May, but close Saturday, June to September.
The opening times of museums is just a rough guide; some are open
longer hours in summer while hours are reduced in winter. Some museums
close at weekends or another day in the week.

## ELECTRICITY

The power supply in Mallorca is:
220–225 volts.

Sockets accept two-pin
plugs (round-pin style),
so an adaptor is needed
for most non-
Continental appliances and a
transformer for appliances operating
on ___ 20 volts.

88

## TIPS/GRATUITIES

| Yes ✓   No ✗ | | |
|---|---|---|
| Restaurants (if service not included) | ✓ | 10% |
| Cafés/bars (if service not included) | ✓ | change |
| Tour guides | ✓ | €1 |
| Hairdressers | ✓ | change |
| Taxis | ✓ | 10% |
| Chambermaids | ✓ | €1 |
| Porters | ✓ | €1 |
| Theatre/cinema usherettes | ✓ | change |
| Cloakroom attendants | ✓ | change |
| Toilets | ✗ | |

## PUBLIC TRANSPORT

**Trains**
The main railway line connects Palma to Inca with branch lines to Sa Pobla (via Muro) and Manacor (via Sineu and Petra). There are regular trains throughout the day, taking around 35 minutes to Inca and 1 hour to Manacor (☎ 971 752245). Five trains a day leave Palma for Sóller, beginning at 8AM (☎ 971 752051) and connecting with the tram to Port de Sóller. The two railway stations are found close together in Palma, beside Plaça d'Espanya.

**Island Buses**
A comprehensive network of buses connects Palma to Mallorca's main towns, with extra services linking the coastal resorts in summer. Buses out of Palma depart from the bus station on Carrer Eusebi Estada, behind Plaça d'Espanya. Palma has its own network of city buses, which also covers the beach resorts around Palma Bay (☎ 971 214444). Bus No 1 runs from 6am to 2am between the airport, city centre and port.

**Boat Trips**
In summer there are regular boat tours of Palma Bay and excursions from resorts including Cala d'Or, Port de Pollença and Port de Sóller. Some of these go to remote beaches which can only be reached by boat. One trip which runs throughout the year is the journey around the northwest coast from Port de Sóller to Sa Colobra (☎ 971 630170).

**Menorca** Day trips to Menorca can be made on a fast catamaran, which leaves Cala Rajada at 9am daily, arriving at the Menorcan city of Ciutadella in one hour. The return journey leaves Ciutadella at 7.30pm (Cape Balear ☎ 902 100444). There are also daily car ferries to Ciutadella from Port d'Alcúdia (☎ 902 119128).

## CAR RENTAL

The leading inter-national car rental companies have offices at Palma airport and you can book a car in advance (essential in peak periods) either direct or through a travel agent. Local companies offer competitive rates and will usually deliver a car to the airport.

## TAXIS

Taxis can be hired at ranks (indicated by a blue square with a 'T'), on the street (by flagging down those with a green light), or at hotels. They are good value within Palma but expensive over long distances. A list of tariffs is displayed at taxi ranks.

## CONCESSIONS

**Students** Holders of an International Student Identity Card may be able to obtain some concessions on travel, entrance fees etc, but Mallorca is not really geared up for students, it is more suited to families and senior citizens. However, there are two youth hostels on the island, one near Palma and the other outside Alcúdia. Another cheap form of accommodation is to stay in a monastery; just turn up or book ahead.

**Senior Citizens** Mallorca is an excellent destination for older travellers, especially in winter when the resorts are quieter, prices more reasonable and hotels offer very economical long-stay rates. The best deals are available through tour operators who specialise in holidays for senior citizens.

## DRIVING

Speed limits on motorways (*autopistas*): 120kph

Speed limits on dual carriageways: 100kph
Speed limits on main roads: 90kph

Speed limits on urban roads: 50kph

Seat belts must be worn at all times. Children under 12 must use a child seat.

Random breath-testing. ...st drive under the influence of alcohol.

All hire cars take either unleaded petrol (*sin plomo*) or diesel (*gasoleo*). The top grade is *Super Plus* (98-octane), though *Super* (96-octane) is usually acceptable. Petrol stations are normally open 6am–10pm, and closed Sundays, though larger ones (often self-service) are open 24 hours. Most take credit cards. There are few petrol stations in the mountain areas.

If you break down driving your own car and are a member of an AIT-affiliated motoring club, you can call the Real Automóvil Club de España (☎ 900 118118 or 917 715140). If the car is hired follow the instructions given in the documentation; most of the international rental firms provide a rescue service.

## PHOTOGRAPHY

**What to photograph**: mountains, hilltop monasteries, pretty villages and attractive harbours.
**Best time to photograph**: the Mallorcan summer sun can be powerful at the height of the day making photos taken at this time appear 'flat'; it is best to photograph in the early morning or late evening.
**Film and camera batteries** are available from shops and *droguerías*.

## PERSONAL SAFETY

The national police force, the Policía Nacional (brown uniforms) keeps law and order in urban areas. Some resorts have their own tourist-friendly Policía Turística. If you need a police station ask for *la comisaría*.

To help prevent crime:
- Do not carry more cash than you need.
- Do not leave valuables on the beach or poolside.
- Beware of pickpockets in markets, tourist sights or crowded places.
- Avoid walking alone in dark alleys at night.

**Police assistance:**
☎ **112**
from any call box

## TELEPHONES

Most public telephones accept coins, credit cards and telephone cards (*tarjetas telefónicas*), available from post offices, news kiosks and tobacconists. Telephone numbers in Mallorca begin with 971; you must dial all nine digits wherever you are calling from. To call Mallorca from the UK dial 00 34; from the USA dial 011 34. To call the operator dial 002.

| International Dialling Codes | |
|---|---|
| From Mallorca (Spain) to: | |
| UK: | 00 44 |
| Germany: | 00 49 |
| USA: | 00 1 |
| Netherlands: | 00 31 |

## POST

**Post Offices**
Post Offices (*correus*) are generally open Mon–Fri, 9am–2pm, but some are also open in the afternoon and on Saturday morning. The main post office in Palma, at Carrer de Constitució 5, is open Mon–Fri, 8.30–8.30, Sat 9am–2pm ☎ 902 197197

## HEALTH

 **Insurance**
Nationals of EU and certain other countries can get medical treatment in Spain with the European Health Insurance Card (EHIC), which has replaced the Form E111, although private medical insurance is still advised and is essential for all other visitors.

 **Dental Services**
Dental treatment is not usually available free of charge as all dentists practise privately. A list of *dentistas* can be found in the yellow pages of the telephone directory. Dental treatment should be covered by private medical insurance.

 **Sun Advice**
The sunniest (and hottest) months are July and August with an average of 11 hours of sun a day and daytime temperatures of 29°C. During these months especially you should avoid the midday sun and use a strong sunblock.

 **Drugs**
Prescription and non-prescription drugs and medicines are available from pharmacies (*farmàcies*), distinguished by a large green cross. Pharmacists are able to dispense many drugs which would be available only on prescription in other countries.

 **Safe Water**
Tap water is generally safe though it can be heavily chlorinated. Mineral water is cheap to buy and is sold as *con gas* (carbonated) and *sin gas* (still). Drink plenty of water during hot weather.

### LANGUAGE

The language that you hear on the streets is most likely to be Mallorquín, a version of Catalan, which itself shares features with both French and Spanish but sounds nothing like either and is emphatically a language, not a dialect. Catalan and Spanish both have official status on Mallorca, and though Spanish will certainly get you by (it is still the language used by Mallorcans to address strangers), it is useful to know some Catalan, if only to understand all those street signs which are being slowly replaced by signs in Catalan.

| | | | |
|---|---|---|---|
| hotel | hotel | chambermaid | cambrera |
| bed and breakfast | llit i berenar | bath | bany |
| single room | habitació senzilla | shower | dutxa |
| double room | habitació doble | toilet | toaleta |
| one person | una persona | balcony | balcó |
| one night | una nit | key | clau |
| reservation | reservas | lift | ascensor |
| room service | servei d'habitació | sea view | vista al mar |

| | | | |
|---|---|---|---|
| bank | banc | credit card | carta de crèdit |
| exchange office | oficina de canvi | exchange rate | tant per cent |
| post office | correus | commission charge | comissió |
| coin | moneda | cashier | caixer |
| banknote | bitllet de banc | change | camvi |
| cheque | xec | foreign currency | moneda estrangera |
| travellers' cheque | xec de viatge | cheap/expensive | barat(a)/car(a) |

| | | | |
|---|---|---|---|
| café | cafè | starter | primer plat |
| pub/bar | celler | main course | segón plat |
| breakfast | berenar | dessert | postres |
| lunch | dinar | bill | cuenta |
| dinner | sopar | beer | cervesa |
| table | mesa | wine | vi |
| waiter | cambrer | water | aigua |
| waitress | cambrera | coffee | cafè |

| | | | |
|---|---|---|---|
| aeroplane | avió | single ticket | senzill-a |
| airport | aeroport | return ticket | anar i tornar |
| train | tren | non-smoking | no fumar |
| bus | autobús | car | cotxe |
| station | estació | petrol | gasolina |
| boat | vaixell | bus stop | la parada |
| port | port | how do I get to...? | per anar a...? |
| ticket | bitllet | where is...? | on és...? |

| | | | |
|---|---|---|---|
| yes | sí | you're welcome | de res |
| no | no | how are you? | com va? |
| please | per favor | do you speak English? | parla anglès? |
| thank you | gràcies | I don't understand | no ho entenc |
| welcome | de res | how much? | quant es? |
| hello | hola | open | obert |
| goodbye | adéu | closed | tancat |
| good morning | bon dia | today | avui |
| good afternoon | bona tarda | tomorrow | demà |
| goodnight | bona nit | right | a la dreta |
| excuse me | perdoni | left | a l'esquerra |

### REMEMBER

- Contact the airport on the day prior to leaving to ensure the flight details are unchanged.

- If travelling by ferry you must check in no later than the time specified on the ticket.

- Spanish customs officials are usually polite and willing to help.

# Index

## A

accommodation 70–73
Acuàrium de Mallorca 56
Alcúdia 24
Andratx 18
Aqualand el Arenal 56
Aqualand Magaluf 56
Arab Baths 53
arriving 87
Artà 25

## B

Badia de Palma 26
Balearic Islands 8, 11
Banyalbufar 18, 58
Banys Àrabs 53
bars 79
Basílica de Sant Francesc 53
Bellver Castle 35
birdwatching 21, 42
Bóquer valley 40
bullfighting 83
Bunyola 16

## C

Cala de Deià 30
Cala Figuera 54
Cala Mondragó 54
Cala de Sant Vicenç 55
Cala d'Or 54
Cala Torta 25
Cala Tuent 43
Camí de S'Arxiduc 19
Ca'n Gordiola 59
Ca'n Solleric 59
Cap de Cala Figuera 26
Cap de Formentor 21, 27
Cap de Ses Salines 21
Cap Gros 55
Capdepera 50
Capocorb Vell 53
car rental 89
Castell d'Alaró 28
Castell de Bellver 35
cellers 65
children 57
children's activities 56–57
Ciutat Romà 24
Chopin, Frédéric 6, 48

clay whistles 76
climate 8
coffee 69
Coll de Sóller 46
concessions 89
consulates 87
Costa Nord 9, 78
Coves d'Artà 29
Coves del Drac 58
craft fairs 77
crafts 76–77
credit cards 75, 87
cricket 83
Cúber reservoir 21, 44
customs 87

## D

Deià 30
dinner shows 80
discos 80
Dragon Caves 58
dress code 64
drives
 central plain 15
 western Mallorca 18
driving in Mallorca 89

## E

eating out 60, 62–69
electricity 88
Els Blauets choir 33
Els Calderers 15
En Fumat 27
entertainment 78–83
Ermita de Bonany 52
Ermita de Sant Llorenç 43
Es Capdella 18
Estellencs 18
Exotic Parque 56

## F

festivals and events 22
fincas 73
fish and seafood 67
football 83
Formentor 27
Fornalutx 50
free attractions 59
Fundació la Caixa 36
Fundació Pilar i Joan Miró

31

## G

Galilea 18, 50
garrigue 20
Gaudí, Antoni 33, 37
geography 8
glass factory and museum 59
golf 81
Golf Fantasia 57
Gorg Blau reservoir 21, 44
Graves, Robert 30
Green Park 57

## H

health 90
health documentation 86
Hidropark 56
history of Mallorca 10–11
hotel grading 70

## I

Inca 51

## J

Jardins de Alfábia 58

## L

La Granja 18, 32
La Seu 37
Lake Martel 58
language 8, 91
Llubí 15
Lluc 33
Llull, Ramón 9, 41, 53

## M

Magaluf 26
maquis 20
Marineland 57
markets 45, 74
mini-golf 57
Mirador des Colomer 27
Mirador de Ses Animes 18
Miró, Joan 9, 31, 38
modernista architecture 36, 46
monastic accommodation 72

money 87
Montuïri 15
Muro 15, 51
Museu de Mallorca 53
Museu de Sóller 46
Museu Etnòlogic de
    Mallorca 51
Museu Junípero Serra 59
Museu Monogràfic de
    Pollentia 24

**N**
national holidays 88
Natural Science Museum
    46
Natura Parc 57
Nemo Submarines 57

**O**
olives 68
opening hours 75, 88
Oratori de Nostra Senyora
    de Gràcia 41
Orient 51

**P**
Palau de l'Almudaina 38
Palma 12, 14, 16, 34–38,
    53
Palma Bay 26
Palma Nova 54
Parc de la Mar 58
passeig 59
passports 86
pearls, cultured 59
Perlas Majórica 59, 76, 77
personal safety 90
Petra 15, 51
photography 89
police 90
Pollença 39
population 8
Port d'Alcúdia 54
Port d'Andratx 54
Port de Pollença 40
Port de Sóller 55
Portals Nous 26
Porto Cristo 55
Porto Petro 54
Post Offices 90

public transport 89
Puig de Galatzó 18
Puig Major 44
Puig de Maria 39, 52
Puig Massanella 44
Puig de Randa 41
Puig de Santa Eugènia
    17
Puigpunyent 50

**R**
Reial Cartoixa 48
Reis de Mallorca 71
Royal Carthusian
    Monastery 48

**S**
Sa Calobra 43
Sa Dragonera 55
Sa Pobla 15, 51
Sa Trapa 55
Safari-Zoo 57
sailing 82
S'Albufera 21, 42
Salines de Llevant 21
Salvator, Archduke
    Ludwig 19, 47
Sand, George 6, 48
Sant Elm 55
Sant Joan 15
Santa Eugènia 17
Santa Maria del Camí
    17
Santuari de Cura 41
Santuari de Sant Honorat
    41
Santuari de Sant Salvador
    52
S'Arenal 26
S'Arracó 55
scuba diving 82
Serra de Tramuntana 12,
    20, 21, 44
Serra, Junípero 9, 51, 52,
    59
Ses Coves 17
Ses Païsses 53
Ses Salines 21
Ses Voltes 59
S'Estació 45

shopping 74–77
S'Hort del Rei 38
Sineu 12, 15, 45
siurells 76
slingshot 83
Sóller 12, 16, 46
Son Marroig 47
sports 83

**T**
Talaiotic culture 53
talaiots 53
tapas 63
taxis 89
Teix 19
telephones 90
theatres and concerts
    78
theme parks and
    waterparks 56
time 86, 87
tips and gratuities 88
Thomás, Catalina 48
Torrent de Pareis 43
tourism 8
tourist offices 86, 88
train and tram tour 16
travel documents 86
travellers' cheques 75, 87
trotting races 83

**V**
Valldemossa 12, 19, 48, 78
visas 86

**W**
walking 20–21
walks
    Archduke's bridlepath
    19
    from Santa Eugènia 17
    Palma 14
water-skiing 82
watersports 82
weather 86
windsurfing 82
wines 60

**Z**
zoos and animals 56–57

# TwinPack
## Mallorca

**Written** Tony Kelly
**Updated by** Mona King
**Designed and produced by** AA Publishing
**Revision management by** Apostrophe S Limited
**Series editor** Cathy Hatley

A CIP catalogue record for this book is available from the British Library.

**ISBN 978-0-7495-4341-9**

Published by AA Publishing, a trading name of Automobile Association Developments Limited, whose registered office is Fanum House, Basing View, Basingstoke, Hampshire RG21 4EA. Registered number 1878835.

Colour separation by Keenes, Andover
Printed and bound by Times Publishing Limited, Malaysia

**ACKNOWLEDGEMENTS**
All pictures used in this publication are held in the Association's own library (AA PHOTO LIBRARY) and were taken by Peter Baker with the exception of the following: JAINIE COWHAM back cover (tram); KEN PATERSON front cover (g) rubber ring, 1, 5a, 6, 13b, 17, 19, 21, 23a, 24a, 25a, 26, 27b, 28b, 29a, 29b, 30b, 31b, 33, 34, 35b, 36a, 36b, 37b, 39a, 41b, 42b, 44b, 45a, 47a, 47b, 49a, 54, 55, 59, 60, 61a, 90t; JEAN-FRANÇOIS PIN front cover (f) jet skier; HEATHER RAINBOW 41a; CLIVE SAWYER Back cover t (monastary), ct (shopping bags), cb (table); ROY VICTOR front cover (b) cocktail; WYN VOYSEY front cover bottom fishing net 12a, 48a

A02696
Fold out map © Freytag-Berndt u. Artaria KG, 1231 Vienna-Austria, all rights reserved

**TITLES IN THE TWINPACK SERIES**
• Algarve • Corfu • Costa Blanca • Costa del Sol • Cyprus • Gran Canaria •
• Lanzarote & Fuerteventura • Madeira • Mallorca • Malta & Gozo • Menorca • Tenerife •

**PUBLISHED IN SPRING 2007**
• Crete
• Croatia

# Dear **TwinPack** Traveller

**Your comments, opinions and recommendations are very important to us. So please help us to improve our travel guides by taking a few minutes to complete this simple questionnaire.**

*You do not need a stamp (unless posted outside the UK). If you do not want to cut this page from your guide, then photocopy it or write your answers on a plain sheet of paper.*

*Send to:* **The Editor, AA TwinPack Travel Guides, FREEPOST SCE 4598, Basingstoke RG21 4GY.**

## Your recommendations…

We always encourage readers' recommendations for restaurants, nightlife or shopping – if your recommendation is used in the next edition of the guide, we will send you a **FREE AA TwinPack Guide** of your choice. Please state below the establishment name, location and your reasons for recommending it.

_____

_____

_____

_____

Please send me **AA TwinPack**

Algarve ☐ Corfu ☐ Costa Blanca ☐ Costa del Sol ☐ Crete ☐
Croatia ☐ Cyprus ☐ Gran Canaria ☐ Lanzarote & Fuerteventura ☐
Madeira ☐ Mallorca ☐ Malta & Gozo ☐ Menorca ☐ Tenerife ☐
(*please tick as appropriate*)

## About this guide…

Which title did you buy?
AA *TwinPack* _____

Where did you buy it? _____

When? m m / y y

Why did you choose an AA *TwinPack* Guide? _____

_____

_____

_____

Did this guide meet your expectations?

Exceeded ☐ Met all ☐ Met most ☐ Fell below ☐

Please give your reasons _____

_____

_____

*continued on next page…*

Were there any aspects of this guide that you particularly liked? _____

_____

_____

Is there anything we could have done better? _____

_____

_____

## About you…

Name (*Mr/Mrs/Ms*) _____

    Address _____

_____

_____ Postcode _____

    Daytime tel no _____

Please only give us your mobile phone number if you wish to hear from us about other products and services from the AA and partners by text or mms.

Which age group are you in?

    Under 25 ☐   25–34 ☐   35–44 ☐   45–54 ☐   55–64 ☐   65+ ☐

How many trips do you make a year?

    Less than one ☐   One ☐   Two ☐   Three or more ☐

Are you an AA member? Yes ☐   No ☐

## About your trip…

When did you book? m m / y y     When did you travel? m m / y y

How long did you stay? _____

Was it for business or leisure? _____

Did you buy any other travel guides for your trip? _____

    If yes, which ones? _____

Thank you for taking the time to complete this questionnaire. Please send it to us as soon as possible, and remember, you do not need a stamp (*unless posted outside the UK*).

*Happy Holidays!*